ORLAND PARK PUBLIC LIBRARY

P9-CNI-073

16 EXTRAORDINARY
NATIVE AMERICANS

NANCY LOBB

J. WESTON
WALCH
PUBLISHER
Portland, Maine

ORLAND PARK PUBLIC LIBRARY

973.04
LoP

Photo Credits

Mary Musgrove:	Hargrett Rare Book and Manuscript Library/University of Georgia Libraries
Tecumseh:	North Wind Picture Archives
Sequoyah:	North Wind Picture Archives
Sacagawea:	Library of Congress LC-USZ62-93141
Sitting Bull:	North Wind Picture Archives
Chief Joseph:	North Wind Picture Archives
Sara Winnemucca:	Courtesy of Nevada State Museum, Carson City, Nevada
Ishi:	Library of Congress LC-D6-35
Susan LaFlesche Picotte:	Nebraska State Historical Society
Jim Thorpe:	AP Wide World Photos
Maria Martinez:	AP Wide World Photos
Annie Dodge Wauneka:	Cecil Stoughton, LBJ Library Collection
N. Scott Momaday:	Nancy Crampton, New York, NY
Ben Nighthorse Campbell:	Office of U.S. Senator, Ben Nighthorse Campbell
Wilma Mankiller:	AP Wide World Photos
Fred Begay:	Los Alamos National Laboratory

1   2   3   4   5   6   7   8   9   10

ISBN 0-8251-3342-4
Copyright © 1997
J. Weston Walch, Publisher
P. O. Box 658 • Portland, Maine 04104-0658
Printed in the United States of America

Contents

Introduction

Let me be a free man—free to travel, free to stop, free to work, free to trade where I choose, free to choose my own teachers, free to follow the religion of my fathers, free to think and talk and act for myself—and I will obey every law, or submit to the penalty. Whenever the white man treats the Indian as they treat each other, then we will have no more wars. We shall all be alike— brothers of one father and one mother, with one sky above us and one country around us and one government for all.

—*Chief Joseph*

The lives of many Native Americans have made a difference in America. Writers, artists, scientists, teachers, politicians, ministers, lawyers, doctors, businesspeople, athletes—all have helped make America what it is.

Native Americans can be proud of their heritage. It is a pride all Americans can share. In this book, you will read the stories of 16 of these people:

- Mary Musgrove, Creek interpreter and diplomat

- Tecumseh, Shawnee warrior and leader

- Sequoyah, Cherokee linguist

- Sacagawea, Shoshone interpreter and guide

- Sitting Bull, Sioux chief and spiritual leader

- Chief Joseph, Nez Percé chief

- Sarah Winnemucca, Paiute Indian rights activist

- Ishi, Yahi survivor and research assistant

- Susan LaFlesche Picotte, Omaha physician

- Jim Thorpe, Sauk and Fox athlete

- Maria Martinez, Pueblo potter

- Annie Dodge Wauneka, Navajo health educator

- N. Scott Momaday, Kiowa poet and writer

- Ben Nighthorse Campbell, Cheyenne, U.S. Senator

- Wilma Mankiller, Chief of the Cherokee nation

- Fred Begay, Navajo nuclear physicist

Where did the Native Americans come from?

Today, Alaska and Siberia are separated by the Bering Strait. The strait is a narrow waterway. It is only 55 miles across at one point. It is shallow—only 90 to 160 feet deep.

During the Ice Age, 10,000 years ago, the whole area was frozen over. Hunters followed game east across the "land bridge." Over the years, they moved south.

Many scientists believe these hunters were the ancestors of the Native Americans. But many Native Americans disagree. Ancient legends tell how the Indian people were created in the New World by divine power.

We know little about the lives of the first Americans. Drawings on stone (pictographs) give some details. But most clues come from objects these people made and used.

By A.D. 1000, many small groups of Indians lived all across America. These groups had different languages, religious beliefs, and customs. Their lives fit their surrondings.

Before 1492, Native Americans numbered 15 to 30 million. They were strong in body and spirit. But the arrival of strangers from across the sea changed their lives.

What happened when people from Europe arrived?

Columbus arrived in the New World in 1492. He thought he had reached India. So he called the Native Americans "Indians." *

More Europeans arrived. They treated the Indians with respect. They knew the Indians had first rights to the land. Any treaties that they made were made as between equals. At the time, the Europeans were still few in number. So, to survive, they needed to be friends with the Indians.

The Indians welcomed the newcomers. They showed them how to survive in the new land. They taught them how to find food and shelter. Had they not, the newcomers probably would have died.

But before long, the settlers began trying to "civilize" the Indians. They taught them their customs and religion. Soon, they began taking more and more of the land. Then the diseases they brought wiped out entire Indian villages. There was smallpox, measles, whooping cough, chicken pox, and the plague. These and other diseases killed as many as 90 percent of the Indians. By the end of the 1600's, eastern tribes had been greatly weakened.

By the 1700's, fur trading thrived in North America. Traders gave the Indians guns and steel tools. The Indians gave the traders furs. In time, the fur animals were gone. Soon, the traders wanted land, too. The Indians were squeezed out.

In the American Revolution, most Indians sided with the English. When the English were defeated, the Indians were punished. More land was taken from them.

Again in the War of 1812, most Indians again sided with the English. The death of their leader Tecumseh ended uprisings in the east. The Indian Removal Policy of 1830 sent most of the Southeast tribes to Oklahoma.

---

* Today, both the terms *American Indian* and *Native American* are common. Both are used in this book. *Native American* describes the group well. *Indian* is shorter and is used in the names of many native groups.

Traders and settlers moved west of the Mississippi River. The diseases they brought killed huge numbers of Indians. White hunters killed the buffalo—the Indian's food supply. The discovery of gold brought more whites westward.

From 1850 to 1880, the plains were full of warfare. The Indians fought to save their land and way of life. But it was a hopeless fight. It was a holocaust—a mass slaughter. By 1890, only 250,000 Native Americans were left. The remaining Indians were forced onto reservations.

Who are the Native Americans today?

After 1900, the number of Indians began to grow. Yet, even today, the number is low. A recent census showed 1,959,234 Native Americans. That is less than 1 percent of the U.S. population.

The census showed about 500 tribes. Of these, 90 percent had fewer than 10,000 people. The largest were the Cherokee, Navajo, Sioux, Chippewa, Choctaw, Pueblo, Iroquois, Apache, Lumbee, and Creek.

People with Indian ancestry are proud of their heritage. Many who are only 1/32 Indian ask to be placed on tribal roles. Native Americans feel they are part of two worlds. And they wish to have the best of both.

Where do Native Americans live today?

Most Native Americans live west of the Mississippi River. The 10 states with the most American Indians are Alaska, New Mexico, Oklahoma, South Dakota, Montana, Arizona, North Dakota, Wyoming, Washington, and Nevada.

Today, 35 percent of Native Americans live on reservations. The reservations cover 54 million acres. The largest reservation is that of the Navajo Indians. It spreads over parts of Arizona, New Mexico, and Utah.

What problems face Native Americans today?

By the end of the nineteenth century, the Indians had lost out. Gone were most their lands and their way of life. Their children had been put in boarding schools. There, they were taught the ways of white society. They were not allowed to speak their language or practice their ceremonies.

Indians on reservations often had no way to earn a living. They had little education. And there were no jobs on the reservation. Their land was often too poor to grow food. Many Indians lived in poverty. Many developed problems with alcohol.

Today, some Native Americans still struggle with these problems. Many, however, combine the best of both worlds in their lives. They have become successful in many careers. Yet, they also have kept close to their native roots and traditions. The 16 Native Americans profiled in this book are outstanding examples.

The motto on the Great Seal of the United States reads *E Pluribus Unum.* That is Latin for "Out of many, one." The United States is made up of many peoples of many races. These peoples have come together to form one nation. Each group has been an important part of American history. I hope you will enjoy reading about 16 Native Americans who have made a difference.

—Nancy Lobb

Mary Musgrove
Creek Interpreter and Diplomat

The Creek Indians were once known as the Muskogee. They built their villages along the creeks and rivers in what is now Alabama and Georgia. When the first English settlers arrived, they called these Indians "Creeks."

In the 1600's, people from England, Spain, and France were exploring the New World. Soon, a race was on to see who could claim the most land for their country.

Sitting right in the middle of this race were the Creek Indians. The Spanish had claimed Mexico. They had moved north into Florida. The French had eastern Canada. They were moving south. And the English had colonies along the Atlantic coast, from Massachusetts to the Carolinas.

Mary Musgrove

The Europeans found the Creeks to be a powerful tribe. Each of the three groups hoped to make the Creeks their allies. Early on, the Creeks became friends with the English.

One Creek woman, Mary Musgrove, played a big part in this friendship. For years she was a friend and interpreter for the English and the Creeks. Her power with both groups was strong. She kept the peace. She was one of the most famous Native

American women of colonial times. She has a place of honor in the history of Georgia.

Musgrove was born around 1700 in the Creek village of Coweta. (This town was in what is now Alabama.) Her Indian name was Coosaponakeesa. She was the daughter of a chief.

A bright child, she was sent to an English school in South Carolina at seven. There, she learned to read and write English. She was baptized and given the name Mary.

She married when she was 16. Her husband was the half-Indian son of an English colonel. The couple moved to Georgia. They had one child. They opened a trading post on Yamacraw Bluff, near the Savannah River. A small band of Creek Indians under Chief Tomochichi lived nearby.

The trading post did well. English goods came from Charleston. The Indians brought thousands of pounds of deer-skins to sell. Soon the Musgroves were living very well.

At the same time, important things were happening in England. In 1732, King George II granted a charter for a new colony. The colony was to be named Georgia in his honor. Its governor was to be James Oglethorpe.

The new colony had raw materials for English industries. It also was a buffer zone between the Carolinas and the Spanish in Florida. It was a place where England sent its citizens who were jobless or in debt.

On February 12, 1733, a group of 114 colonists arrived at Yamacraw. (It was later renamed Savannah.) They were met by Chief Tomochichi, the Musgroves, and a band of Indians.

Mary Musgrove was the interpreter. Tomochichi and Oglethorpe signed the Treaty of 1733. The treaty said that the English could build a town at Savannah. The Creeks agreed to let the English settle on other land. In return, the English agreed to send traders to the Creek villages. The two groups agreed to be friends.

Oglethorpe thought the rest of the Creek nation should have a chance to sign the treaty. Musgrove called 50 Creek chiefs to Savannah. After several meetings, the chiefs signed the treaty.

Oglethorpe knew that his people had to be friends with the Indians to survive. Mary Musgrove made sure that this friendship grew. She could speak English and several Indian languages. So, Oglethorpe made her his interpreter and go-between.

In 1734, Oglethorpe decided that the Treaty of 1733 should be approved in England. A group set out by ship. Tomochichi, now a friend of Oglethorpe's, went along. Musgrove's husband went as interpreter. Mary Musgrove stayed home to mind the trading post.

Oglethorpe hoped to impress the Indians with the power of England. Indeed, they were amazed at how the English lived. The people lived so close together. Also, England had a lot of noise, bad smells, and many big buildings. After four months, the group returned to Georgia. Tomochichi thought the English lifestyle was grand. But he knew the Indians lived much more happily.

In 1735, Musgrove's husband died. The next year Mary Musgrove married an Indian trader. Oglethorpe asked Musgrove to open a new trading post farther south. This new post at Mount Venture was important because it was close to the Florida border. There, Musgrove worked to watch and protect the colony's southern borders.

Musgrove worked to keep the Creek-English friendship alive. She arranged meetings between the two groups. In 1739, a meeting of the Creek nation took place in Coweta. Musgrove invited Oglethorpe.

Oglethorpe rode 300 miles on horseback through the wilderness. He was royally received by the Indians. For 10 days they feasted and talked. The Creeks spoke about their problems with the English. Oglethorpe settled the problems. The Creeks agreed to stay loyal to the English. The Treaty of 1733 was renewed.

In 1739, the Spanish and English clashed in a border war. Oglethorpe asked Mary Musgrove for help from the Indians. Musgrove called for 1,000 warriors. The Spanish were defeated. They went back to Florida. They did not attack Georgia again.

In 1742, Musgrove and her husband returned to Savannah. That summer, he died. Meanwhile, Spanish Indians nearly destroyed the trading post at Mount Venture. Musgrove stayed in Savannah. She continued her work with the Indians.

Oglethorpe served in Georgia for 10 years. He returned to England in 1743. His partnership with Musgrove ended.

The two had worked together well. When threats from the Spanish or French arose Musgrove got Oglethorpe help from the Indians. When problems between the Creeks and English arose, Musgrove settled them. Oglethorpe trusted and depended on her. She never let him down.

Before he left, Oglethorpe gave Musgrove a diamond ring and 200 pounds (English money). He also promised her 100 pounds a year to serve as interpreter for the new governor. He even hoped to pay for her losses (at Mount Venture).

In 1744, Musgrove married again. Her third husband was greedy. He was also in debt. His power over her was not good. He involved her in a plan to pay off his debts.

He told Musgrove that she had not been paid enough for her services to Georgia. He got her to ask for land. She claimed three coastal islands, plus land near Savannah. She said that all had been promised to her by Tomochichi (now dead). This claim was clearly untrue. Musgrove also demanded a large amount of money.

To get these huge payments, Musgrove, her husband, and a group of warriors threatened the people in Savannah. The suitation became tense. Musgrove and her husband were jailed for a few days. The chiefs calmed down and went home.

Musgrove and her husband continued their fight in court. The case dragged on for 13 years. It was clear that their claims were too large. Yet, Musgrove had served the colony well. She deserved some reward.

Finally, a compromise was reached. Musgrove was paid 2,050 pounds. She was also given St. Catherine's Island. She and her husband built a house on the island. From there, she worked to keep the Creeks and the English friendly. In 1763, she died. She was buried on the island.

Musgrove did cause trouble at the end. But she played a key role in Georgia's history. Her diplomacy helped keep the colony's early years peaceful.

Musgrove's work during the war with the Spanish was vital. Because of her, the Creeks stood firm between the two sides. Thus, the colony did not become Spanish land. Mary Musgrove has been called by some the Savior of Georgia.

Remembering the Facts

1. Where did the Creek Indians get their name?

2. Why was the Creek nation important in colonial times?

3. What were the terms of the Treaty of 1733?

4. The Musgroves' first trading post was opened at the site of what future city?

5. What key things did Mary Musgrove do in the first two years of the colony?

6. Why did Musgrove open a second trading post at Mount Venture?

7. What happened at the 1739 meeting in Coweta?

8. How did Musgrove help the English in the Spanish-English war of 1739?

9. What payment did Oglethorpe give Musgrove for her services as interpreter?

10. What land was Musgrove finally given as payment?

Understanding the Story

11.   What do you think might have happened if the Creeks had been unfriendly to the English colonists?

12.   In what ways do you think the Creek-English friendship helped both sides?

Getting the Main Idea

Why do you think Mary Musgrove has an honored role in the history of Georgia?

Applying What You've Learned

Imagine you are there in 1739 as Mary Musgrove gives a speech. She is asking the Creeks to join the fight against the Spanish. Write a paragraph telling what you "hear" her say.

Tecumseh
Shawnee Warrior and Leader

It was the summer of 1810. The streets of Vincennes, in the Indiana Territory, were filled with soldiers. Governor William Henry Harrison sat on the porch of the governor's mansion. With him were many of the town's leading citizens. Excitement filled the air.

Tecumseh

Tecumseh strode through the crowd. With him were many Shawnee warriors. The warriors had paint on their faces and feathers in their hair. The whites and the Indians were having yet another peace talk.

Both Tecumseh and Harrison were strong leaders. Tecumseh was known for his bravery and leadership in battle. He had gotten Indians of many nations to join him in resisting the whites. Now, he was acting as their spokesperson. Harrison was a famous Indian fighter. He was later elected the ninth president of the United States.

Tecumseh spoke first:

> Once, [the Indians] were a happy race. Now, they are made miserable by the white people, who are never contented but forever [greedy]. The only way to stop this evil is for all the red men to unite in claiming an equal right to the land. The land belongs to all, for the use of everyone. No groups among us have a right to sell, even to one another, much less to

strangers who want all and will not do with less. Sell a country!
Why not sell the air, the clouds, and the great sea, as well as
sell the earth?

At the end of this speech, there was silence. Finally, Harrison rose to reply. He began telling of how fairly the Indians had been treated. Tecumseh shouted, "He lies!" Both sides drew their weapons. But there was no fight that day. Harrison withdrew to his mansion. The Indians walked off. Once again, no agreement was reached. But the two men would meet again.

Tecumseh was born in 1768 in Old Piqua. This Shawnee village was in what is now western Ohio. It was a beautiful country of fertile land. But whites started coming in growing numbers. They cleared the land. They put up fences. Soon much of the game was chased away.

Clashes between whites and Indians became common. When Tecumseh was seven, his father was killed in battle. When Tecumseh was 11, the village was attacked. After that, nearly 1,000 Shawnees moved to Missouri. Tecumseh's mother was among them. But Tecumseh stayed, in the care of his older brother.

When Tecumseh was 14, he began fighting with Shawnee war parties. He became known as a brave and skillful fighter. But he was also kindhearted. Once, he saw a white prisoner being burned to death. Outraged, he vowed he would never allow such torture. For the rest of his life, he insisted on the humane treatment of prisoners.

In 1776, the Americans defeated the British in the Revolutionary War. The British pulled back to Canada. The United States pursued its dream of expanding westward.

Some Indian chiefs sold land they did not own to the government. These lands were divided into homesteads. The settlers cleared the land for farms.

Battles between the Indians and the U.S. Army increased. Tecumseh became chief of a band of warriors. He fought in many battles. In 1792, the Indians suffered a big defeat. It was at the Battle of Fallen Timbers. The army went on to destroy many Indian villages.

Finally, in 1795, the Indians signed the Treaty of Greenville. This treaty gave most of Ohio and part of Indiana to the government. Tecumseh refused to sign. He moved his band west to Indiana. He became known as the one who had stood up for Indian rights.

Tecumseh began working to unite the Indians. He traveled from tribe to tribe. He spoke to them and tried to win them over to his goals.

Tecumseh wanted all the tribes to join together as a new Indian nation. His plan was for all Indian lands to be owned in common. Tecumseh also hoped to start a free Indian nation in an area between the United States and Canada.

He knew that his plan would require a fight. He began gathering warriors in Tippecanoe, Indiana. Soon he had over 1,000 warriors.

Harrison watched all this with alarm. His greatest wish was to break the Indians. That would make Indiana safe for settlers. Harrison met Tecumseh at Vincennes. The meeting was doomed from the start. Their goals were too opposite.

The peace talks failed. Tecumseh traveled to meet with the chiefs of many tribes. He talked with the Choctaws, Chickasaws, Cherokees, Seminoles, Creeks, Osages, and Iowas. Over and over again, he asked for unity:

> *Where are the Pequots? Where are the Narragansetts? the Mohicans? the Pokanokets and many other once powerful tribes of our people? They have vanished before the [greed] of the white man, as snow before a summer sun. The destruction of our race is at hand, unless we unite in one common cause against the common foe.*

The young men were stirred by these words. They wanted to join Tecumseh. But often they were held back by their elders. Tecumseh made little progress. Discouraged, he returned to Tippecanoe. He found the town had been destroyed.

Harrison had struck while Tecumseh was away. A few Indians were killed. Most had retreated. After the battle, the army burned the town.

It was not a major battle. But the story grew larger with each telling. Years later, it helped elect Harrison president. Harrison's slogan in 1840 was "Tippecanoe and Tyler too!" (John Tyler ran for vice president on the ticket with Harrison.)

After Tippecanoe, the Indians were in disarray. Tecumseh tried to rally his forces. Then, on June 18, 1812, the United States declared war on Great Britain. Both sides tried to get the Indians to join them. Tecumseh allied with the British. He led his warriors in many battles.

One stunning British victory took place at Fort Detroit. The British guns began to shell the fort. From another direction, Tecumseh's warriors marched across a clearing three times. The American general thought that huge numbers of Indians had arrived. The white flag was raised before the attack began.

The settlers were shocked. More and more Indians joined Tecumseh's cause. It looked as if an Indian nation might be formed.

But the tide of the war turned. The British retreated into Canada. The Battle of the Thames, on October 5, 1813, was decisive. The British and Indian forces fought bravely. But they were vastly outnumbered. Tecumseh and many others were killed.

In 1814, the war ended. As part of the peace terms, the British made a request. They asked the Americans to allow an Indian state between the United States and Canada. But the Americans refused to give up any land. And no strong leader spoke for the Indians.

Tecumseh's dream of an Indian nation died with him. Most of the Indians were removed to the other side of the Mississippi River. The young country continued its push westward.

Remembering the Facts

1. Why did the 1810 meeting between Tecumseh and William Henry Harrison end badly?

2. Where was Tecumseh born and raised?

3. Why did Tecumseh's mother leave her children?

4. What were the terms of the Treaty of Greenville?

5. What was Tecumseh's dream?

6. Why did Tecumseh gather warriors at the Tippecanoe River?

7. Why did Harrison use the slogan "Tippecanoe and Tyler too!" in his campaign for the presidency?

8. What happened of the Battle of the Thames?

9. Why couldn't the British help start an Indian nation?

10. Why did Tecumseh's dream of an Indian nation die with him?

Understanding the Story

11. How do you think history might have changed had Tecumseh lived to old age?

12. Harrison respected Tecumseh as a great leader. Once he said of Tecumseh, "If it were not for the closeness of the United States, he would perhaps be the founder of an empire that would rival in glory that of Mexico or Peru." What signs of leadership do you see in Tecumseh's life?

Getting the Main Idea

Why is the story of Tecumseh important to the history of the United States?

Applying What You've Learned

Imagine that Tecumseh's dream of an Indian nation between the United States and Canada had come true. Write a paragraph describing the new nation. Where are its boundaries? Who lives there? What are its customs?

Sequoyah
Cherokee Linguist

A president's yacht. A county seat in Oklahoma. A national park in California. A nuclear power plant in Tennessee. A number of businesses. And the giant redwood trees in California.

What do all these things have in common? All are named after the Indian Sequoyah. This remarkable man invented a written language for the Cherokees. It is an amazing tale.

Sequoyah was born around 1770 in Taskigi, Tennessee. His

Sequoyah

mother's name was Wurteh. She was Cherokee. His father, Nathaniel Gist, was a white trader.

Sequoyah's father left before the boy was born. Sequoyah grew up with no schooling. He spoke no English. A hunting injury left him crippled. He became known as the Lame One. But his mind was quick and active.

Sequoyah was raised as a hunter and trader. Later, he learned to work as a silversmith. He became a fine craftsman. By age 20, he was well known for his beautiful work. He made bracelets, earrings, knife handles, and buttons.

One day, a friend suggested that Sequoyah sign his work. Sequoyah did not know how to write. He asked a friend to help.

The name he gave was George Gist, his white name. The friend misunderstood. He wrote "George Guess." Sequoyah did not know the difference. So he signed his pieces George Guess. This became his trademark.

The death of his mother hit Sequoyah hard. He had to leave the house they had shared. He wandered around Cherokee country. Then he settled in Willstown, Tennessee. There he married Utiya, a Cherokee woman. They had five children.

In the War of 1812, some Cherokees fought on the American side. Sequoyah rode off to fight in Georgia.

Sequoyah watched other soldiers reading letters from home. He saw them smile as they looked at the papers. He wondered how the "talking leaves" worked. He knew that the whites had a power that the Cherokees did not.

The war ended. Sequoyah returned home. But he could not forget the "talking leaves." He began to draw symbols for each word he knew. On bark, he wrote symbol after symbol.

But there were too many words to have a picture for each. Finally, Sequoyah found the key. Many words had the same sounds. He used a different symbol for each sound. Then he could write any word.

Sequoyah spent all his time writing symbols on birch bark. He made progress on his work. But the rest of his life fell apart.

His cabin needed repairs. Rain gushed in through holes in the roof. Sequoyah never noticed. He had no time to work in the fields. His sons tended the crops so that the family could eat. Sequoyah thought of nothing but his work. His friends thought he had lost his mind.

Finally, his wife had had enough. She threw the piles of bark into the fire. Years of work went up in flames. Sequoyah took his daughter Ahyoka and left. He moved into a nearby cabin. There, he worked to remember the symbols he had made.

One day, Sequoyah found an old English speller. He saw that the English alphabet had only 26 letters. His Cherokee alphabet had 200 symbols. So he continued to narrow it down.

There were more problems. Other members of the tribe did not understand Sequoyah's ideas. They thought he was practicing witchcraft. They set fire to his cabin. Once again, all his work was destroyed. This time, Sequoyah remembered the symbols. He wrote them down again. But he knew he had to leave town.

Beginning in 1782, many Cherokees moved west. They settled in what is now Oklahoma and Arkansas. The Cherokee nation was split in two: the Cherokee Nation East and the Cherokee Nation West.

Sequoyah went west in 1817 to make a new life for himself. On his way, he met a Cherokee named Sally. The two were married. They settled in eastern Oklahoma.

Sequoyah kept working on his writing system. By 1821, he had it down to 86 symbols. What he actually developed was a syllabary. A syllabary is different from an alphabet. Each alphabet letter can have several sounds. But each syllabary symbol is always said the same way.

Using the syllabary, Sequoyah taught of his family to read. His system worked! And it was easy to use. Sequoyah wanted to share it with all Cherokees.

First, he needed approval from the tribal council. The council was meeting back east. Sequoyah and his daughter Ahyoka made the long trip.

The council chairman in 1821 was John Ross. He had been to Dartmouth College. He said that Sequoyah could display his syllabary.

Sequoyah sent Ahyoka sent out of the room. Ross whispered a message to Sequoyah. Sequoyah wrote it down. Ahyoka came back into the room. She read the message easily. The council quickly adopted the syllabary. The Cherokees became the first U.S. tribe to have their own writing system.

Sequoyah began teaching his system to his tribe. Soon, thousands of Cherokees could read and write. By 1825, the Bible was printed in Cherokee. In 1828, the *Cherokee Phoenix* newspaper was first published.

Sequoyah was well rewarded for his work. The tribe gave him a yearly pension. They made him a tribal adviser, called an Old

Beloved Man. And they gave him a silver medal. On it were two crossed pipes. These stood for the Eastern and Western Cherokees, brought together by Sequoyah's work.

Sequoyah was growing old. For years, he had heard about a band of Cherokees who had migrated to Mexico. In 1843, he and his son went to search for the lost Cherokees. The trip was too much. The old man died. He was buried in the Mexican state of Tamaulipas. The location of his grave is unknown.

Sequoyah was not a great speaker. He was not a great warrior or hunter. But he gave his people something of great worth: the gift of literacy—the opportunity to read and write. For this he will always be remembered.

Remembering the Facts

1. What craft did Sequoyah learn as a young man?

2. How did Sequoyah get the idea of a written Cherokee language?

3. Why did Sequoyah's first try for a written language fail?

4. What did the tribe first think about Sequoyah's work?

5. Why did Sequoyah move to Oklahoma in 1817?

6. How is a syllabary different from an alphabet?

7. How did Sequoyah win tribal approval for his syllabary?

8. Name two early works written in Cherokee.

9. Why did Sequoyah go to Mexico?

Understanding the Story

10. Why do you think Sequoyah's syllabary was so important to the future of the Cherokee tribe?

11. Why do you think the tribe was so fearful of Sequoyah's early work?

Getting the Main Idea

In what ways do you think Sequoyah is a good role model for young people today?

Applying What You've Learned

Imagine that you are a newspaper reporter. You are covering the tribal council meeting in which Sequoyah first shows his syllabary. Write a newspaper article telling what happens at the meeting. Describe how people feel about the syllabary. Tell the outcome of the meeting.

Sacagawea
Shoshone Interpreter and Guide

In 1803, President Thomas Jefferson bought the Louisiana Territory. He bought it from the French emperor Napoléon. The cost? Three million dollars, or about three cents an acre. This vast area stretched from the Mississippi River to the Rocky Mountains. The purchase doubled the size of the United States.

But the Louisiana Purchase was a gamble. No white man knew what the new land was like. Was it worth the money? Or had Jefferson been tricked?

Sacagawea

To find out, Jefferson sent a team to explore the land. The team's mission was to describe the land and its people, animals, and plants. It was also to search for a water route to the Pacific. The team led by Meriwether Lewis and William Clark.

This was a historic journey. It led to the opening of the American West. Sacagewea played a key role. She was an interpreter and peacekeeper with the Indians. Without her, the mission might not have succeeded.

Sacagawea was around 1784. She was of the Lehmi band of Shoshone Indians. The Shoshones lived in what is now central Idaho. Sacagawea's father was chief of the village.

In 1800, Hidatsa Indians attacked the village. A number of Shoshones were killed. Sacagawea was captured. She was taken to the Hidatsa village near the North Dakota border.

She was sold to French Canadian fur trader Toussaint Charbonneau. He was living among the Hidatsa. He later married Sacagawea.

At the same time, Lewis and Clark were starting their journey. They left St. Louis, Missouri, on May 14, 1804. Five months later, on October 26, they reached the Hidatsa village. They built cabins nearby. And they settled in for the winter. They called their settlement Fort Mandan.

Sacagawea was pregnant. On February 11, 1805, she gave birth to Jean Baptiste Charbonneau. She called him Pomp. This Shoshone name meant "leader."

Spring approached. Lewis and Clark prepared to resume their journey. They hired Charbonneau to act as an interpreter. There was one condition. He must bring his wife, Sacagawea.

Sacagawea knew the languages and customs of western tribes. She could interpret and negotiate. Also, she would be a sign that the group was peaceful. By Indian law, a woman could not go with a war party.

On April 7, 1805, the party set out. Some walked along the riverbanks. Others rode in canoes. Sacagawea carried her two-month-old son on her back.

Sacagawea quickly proved her worth to the party. On the second day, she found dried roots and wild artichokes. Later, she hunted in the woods for berries. The things she added to the party's meat-and-bread diet helped to keep everyone well. No one was lost on the long trip.

The early part of the trip was peaceful. There was an occasional bear, mountain lion, or rattlesnake. But mosquitoes and other insects proved to be a bigger problem.

The first close call occurred May 14. Charbonneau, Sacagawea, and some others were in the large canoe. Strong winds began to blow. The canoe nearly overturned. Papers, books, medicines, and supplies were washed overboard.

The men fought to steady the canoe. Some panicked. Sacagawea kept her head. She reached into the swirling water.

She caught most of the floating things. In doing so, she very likely saved the expedition and its valuable records. Lewis named a stream after her as thanks.

On June 10, Sacagawea became ill. Both Lewis and Clark tended to her. Nothing worked. Both men feared she might die. At last, Lewis thought of giving her mineral water from a spring they had passed. This worked. Sacagawea recovered.

A few days later, Sacagawea and Pomp nearly drowned in a flash flood. They were walking up a narrow canyon with a group. It began to rain. The group found shelter under a rock outcropping. But heavy rain farther up the canyon unleashed a wall of water. The water came rushing down. The only escape was to climb the canyon's sheer walls. This they were able to do. The water swept by below them. It was a narrow escape.

The journey became more difficult. The canoes ran into rapids and shallow water. Most of the party walked. Everyone got cold, wet, and tired. Lewis wanted to cross the mountains before winter.

On August 17, the party met some Shoshone Indians. To her delight, Sacagawea saw that the chief was her brother Cameahwait. She was able to get nine horses and other supplies for the Lewis and Clark party. She also got her brother and others to guide the party through the mountains.

The group made it across the snowy mountains. They continued by canoe down the Snake and Columbia Rivers. Finally, they reached the Pacific Ocean. Sacagawea took Pomp from her back and held him up to see the mighty waters.

A ship was supposed to meet them there. It was going to take them back to St. Louis. But it never arrived. So the group made camp for the winter. They called their camp Fort Clatsop.

On March 23, 1806, they began the trip home. At one point, the group split up in order to see more land. Sacagawea stayed with the Clark party. Along the Yellowstone River, they passed an unusual rock formation. Clark named it after Pomp: Pompey's Pillar. Clark scratched the name deep into the rock.

On August 14, the party reached Fort Mandan. Three days later, Lewis and Clark returned to St. Louis.

Charbonneau got $500.33 as pay for the expedition. Sacagawea was paid nothing. But Clark gave her a medal. He invited her and Charbonneau live in St. Louis. And he offered to adopt Pomp and send him to the best schools.

Sacagawea went to St. Louis for a time. She left Pomp with Clark to raise. The boy grew up to be an interpreter and mountain man.

The rest of Sacagawea's life is a mystery. There are two theories about what happened to her. Some say that she died on December 20, 1812, at a Missouri River trading post.

Others say that she left Charbonneau and went to live with her people in Wyoming. She remarried and had more children. She became a tribal leader at the Wind River reservation. She was called Porivo, which means "chief." She lived to nearly 100, dying on April 9, 1884. Many people who close to her thought she was the real Sacagawea.

The truth about Sacagawea's death may never be known. But it is certain that she helped the Lewis and Clark Expedition succeed. She served as interpreter and negotiator. She shared her knowledge of plants and animals. Her common sense saved the day many times. Her courage kept the men from losing heart on their 8,000-mile journey.

For a hundred years, Sacagawea was a mere footnote in history. Then, historians became interested in her role. Today, her story is known by every schoolchild. She has been honored by statues and monuments all over the West.

Remembering the Facts

1. What were two reasons for the Lewis and Clark Expedition?
2. Why did Sacagawea go on the journey?
3. Why did a woman help make the expedition safer?
4. How did Sacagawea keep the party in good health?
5. What help did Sacagawea get from the Shoshones for her group?

6. What disappointment happened when the group reached the Pacific Ocean?

7. How did Clark help Pomp?

8. What are the two theories about Sacagawea's death?

Understanding the Story

9. There was little interest in Sacagawea's story until long after her death. Why do you think this was so? Why do you think there was later interest in her story?

10. What problems do you think might have come up if the Lewis and Clark Expedition had not taken Sacagawea?

Getting the Main Idea

Why do you think the Lewis and Clark Expedition was so important in our country's history?

Applying What You've Learned

Imagine that you are a historian. You are trying to unravel the mystery of Sacagawea's death. Where might you look for information? What problems might you have?

Sitting Bull
Sioux Chief and Spiritual Leader

Sitting Bull may be the best-known Indian in history. He was a great warrior and chief. He was also a respected holy man.

In the late 1800's, Sitting Bull fought whites who took Indian land. He is best known for the battle at the Little Bighorn.

The memory of Sitting Bull has inspired generations. He never wavered in the fight to preserve Indian rights.

Sitting Bull was born in the winter of 1831. His parents lived on Willow Creek, in what is now South Dakota. They parents belonged to the Hunkpapa Sioux tribe. This tribe moved from place to place in search of buffalo.

Sitting Bull

Sioux country was harsh. Winter brought fierce cold and great blizzards. Summer brought heat and droughts.

To survive, the Sioux had to be strong. They were a religious people. They believed that the Great Spirit was in all living things. Therefore, they honored the animals around them. They lived in harmony with the earth.

As a child, Sitting Bull never saw a white man. Wagon trains on their way west, followed the Oregon trail. But this was far to the south. No whites had settled in the land of the Sioux.

Sitting Bull was a quiet and serious child. He was careful about everything he did. For this reason, his parents named him

Slow. Some people thought he was slow in the head. But he soon proved them wrong.

At age 10, the boy killed his first buffalo. At 14, he took his first *coup*. A coup was the touching of an enemy warrior with a special stick, and then living to tell about it. Taking coup brought great honor. The boy's father was very proud. At the campfire that evening, he gave Slow a new name: Sitting Bull.

As a youth, Sitting Bull led an elite warrior group called the Strong Hearts. In a battle with the Crows, he got a bullet wound in his left foot. For the rest of his life, he walked with a limp.

In the 1860's, Sitting Bull became chief of the Hunkpapa Sioux. By then, the Hunkpapa had white settlers all around them. To the east, homesteaders flooded the Dakota territory. To the west, gold had been discovered in Montana territory. To the south, settlers were everywhere.

In 1866, the army built Fort Buford in the middle of Hunkpapa territory. Sitting Bull had had enough. He and the Strong Hearts attacked. They roamed hundred of miles, killing settlers and soldiers. Other Sioux groups joined the fight.

By 1868, the U.S. government was ready for peace. The Fort Laramie treaty created a Sioux reservation on a huge part of the Dakota territory. This land included the Black Hills, an area sacred to the Sioux. It also included the Powder River hunting ground in Wyoming. The treaty stated: "No white person shall be permitted to settle upon it, or without consent of the Indians to pass through the same."

Many Sioux chiefs were tired of fighting. They agreed to sign the treaty and live on the reservation.

Sitting Bull refused. He would not sign a treaty that took away Sioux land. He said:

> *The Great Spirit gave us this land, and we are at home here. I will not have my people robbed. I want everyone to know that I do not propose to sell any part of my country.*

Sitting Bull and a few other chiefs stayed off the reservation.

The ink was barely dry before the treaty was being broken. Gold was discovered in the Black Hills. Thousands of people streamed into the area.

The government tried to buy the Black Hills. But no Sioux chief was willing to sell sacred ground. The Indians were furious. Their holy land was being treated with disrespect.

Things were dangerous during the winter of 1875–1876. So, the government ordered all Indians to come onto the reservation. Sitting Bull, Crazy Horse, and other chiefs ignored the order. Instead, they called a war council at Rosebud Creek in southern Montana. By June 1876, 15,000 Indians had gathered. Plans were made to fight the white man.

Before the battle, the Sioux held their sacred sun dance. Sitting Bull, now 45 years old, was a holy man as well as a chief. He asked the Great Spirit for help in the coming battle.

Fifty pieces of flesh were cut from each of Sitting Bull's arms. Then he danced and prayed. After a day and a half, he saw a vision. He saw many white soldiers falling upside down from the sky into the Indian camp. This was a good omen. Sitting Bull announced that the Indians would win a great victory.

A week later, Sitting Bull's vision came true. On June 25, 1876, the Indian camp was attacked by the troops of General George Armstrong Custer. Custer was a famous Indian fighter. But he made a fatal error that day. He and the soldiers with him were crushed.

The Battle of Little Bighorn became known as Custer's Last Stand. It was the worst defeat of the army by the Indians. People everywhere were shocked. The army vowed to break the Indians for good.

The soldiers chased Sitting Bull and his followers into Canada. Winter came. Many chiefs gave up. they went onto the reservation. In May 1877, even Crazy Horse surrendered. (Later that year, at age of 35, he was killed by soldiers.)

The Sioux were not happy in Canada. They were cold and hungry. They missed those who had gone onto the reservation. After four years of exile, Sitting Bull surrendered. Fewer than 200 members of his tribe were left.

To his surprise, Sitting Bull had become the most famous Indian in the country. He was known as the Slayer of Custer. Reporters came to interview him. In 1885, Buffalo Bill Cody talked Sitting Bull into joining his Wild West Show. The show traveled throughout the country. Sitting Bull learned to sign his name.

Then sold his autograph for a quarter. Most of this money he gave to the poor.

Sitting Bull had not forgotten his people. In 1889, the government wanted another chunk of the reservation for settlers. Government agents knew Sitting Bull would never agree. So they went behind his back. They convinced other chiefs to sell 11 million acres. Sitting Bull was furious. "There are no Indians left but me!" he cried.

Indians were losing more than land. Their identity was being taken away. Their children were sent to boarding schools and taught white ways. Indian religious ceremonies were forbidden. Reservation Indians were dying from hunger and disease.

A new religion offered the Indians hope. It promised that the Indians would regain their old way of life. It was called the ghost dance religion.

Indian agents feared that the ghost dance would cause an uprising. If that happened, Sitting Bull was the only chief with enough power to lead it.

Sitting Bull had little to do with the new religion. But on December 15, 1890, Indian police arrested him. They hoped to end the ghost dance. Sitting Bull resisted arrest. Shooting broke out. Sitting Bull and 14 others were killed.

Three hundred Hunkpapa Sioux fled the reservation. They feared they would also be killed. The army caught up to them at a place called Wounded Knee.

It was bitterly cold. The Indians had only a few guns. So they gave up the fight. As they sat in the snow, a shot rang out from somewhere. The army used machine guns and rifles on the unarmed Indians.

Men, women, and children were shot down in the snow. When the Battle of Wounded Knee ended, all but a handful were dead.

This was the end of the Indian wars. Now, all Indians were reservation Indians. And the ghost dance was silenced forever.

But Sitting Bull was not forgotten. He never lost courage defending his people. He refused to quit even when defeat was certain. But he was more than a great warrior. He was the religious leader of his tribe, as well. He was a hero to all people with the will to be free.

Remembering the Facts

1. Why were the Hunkpapa Sioux not fighting the white man when Sitting Bull was a child?

2. How did Sitting Bull get the name Slow?

3. Why did his father honor him by giving him the name Sitting Bull?

4. What did the Fort Laramie treaty give the Sioux?

5. Why did Sitting Bull not agree to the treaty?

6. What vision did Sitting Bull see during the sun dance?

7. Why did Sitting Bull go to Canada?

8. Why was Sitting Bull arrested in 1890?

9. What happened at Wounded Knee?

Understanding the Story

10. Why do you think Sitting Bull said, "There are no Indians left but me"?

11. Why do you think the Wounded Kneed massacre ended Indian resistance?

Getting the Main Idea

There were many great Indian chiefs. Why do you think Sitting Bull is remembered by many as the greatest?

Applying What You've Learned

Imagine that you are a member of a Sioux tribe in 1868. The U.S. government has just offered the Fort Laramie peace treaty. In a tribal meeting, people are discussing whether to accept the treaty and move to the reservation. It is your turn to speak. What do you say?

Chief Joseph
Nez Percé Chief

The Wallowa Valley in Oregon was a paradise. Fifty miles wide, it was circled by tree-covered mountains. The streams were full of salmon. The hills teemed with elk, antelope, and deer. Lake Wallowa shimmered in the valley below.

Chief Joseph

For hundreds of years, a band of Nez Percé Indians had lived in this valley. They hunted, fished, and raised horses and cattle. In the summer, they crossed the mountains into Montana to hunt buffalo.

French fur trappers arrived in the valley around 1750. They were the first whites the Indians had seen. They lived in peace with the Indians. They named them Nez Percé, meaning "pierced nose." Some nearby bands of Indians wore shells as nose ornaments. The Nez Percé never did this. But the name stuck.

Into this happy valley, Joseph was born in 1840. He was named Hin-mah-too-yah-lah-ket. That means "thunder rolling in the mountains." Later, he took the name Joseph.

More white men came to the Wallowa Valley. In 1855, the Nez Percé gave some land to the U.S. government. This did not include the Wallowa Valley. It was to belong to the Nez Percé for all time. The Nez Percé were content. They thought that there was plenty of land for everyone. But they were wrong.

In 1863, a new treaty took much more of the tribe's land. Even the Wallowa Valley was given to the whites. Many of the Nez Percé chiefs refused to sign. They called it the Thief Treaty. One of these was Joseph's father, Old Joseph. These chiefs stayed outside the reservation.

In 1871, Old Joseph died. His last words were to his son, Joseph:

> *You are now the chief of these people. Always remember that your father never sold his country. You must stop your ears whenever you are asked to sign a treaty selling your home. A few years more and white men will be all around you. They have their eyes on this land. My son, never forget my dying words.*

Joseph listened to his father's words. He refused to move onto the reservation.

More settlers moved into the valley. They fenced the land and built roads. Joseph tried to avoid trouble. He moved his people to a remote part of the valley. He was proud that the Nez Percé had never killed a white man.

But things were about to change. On June 10, 1877, President Ulysses S. Grant ordered the Wallowa Valley opened to settlers. General Oliver O. Howard asked the non-treaty Indians to go to the Lapwai reservation in Idaho.

Howard was an honorable man. He was a Civil War hero. He was kind and had a strong sense of justice. He believed that the government had no right to move the Indians from their land. But an army officer must follow orders. Howard ordered Joseph and the others to the reservation.

None of the chiefs wanted a war. They were outnumbered and outgunned. So, they left their homes. They traveled north toward the reservation.

But the young men of the tribes thought their chiefs were cowardly. A group of them returned to the valley. They began killing white settlers. Joseph was away from the camp at the time. He was unaware of their actions.

Howard had to subdue the tribe. The Indians knew they must protect themselves. War could no longer be avoided. They fled to White Bird Canyon. There, they were in a good position in case of attack.

Joseph had never fought a battle. He had always tried to live in peace. But on June 17, 1877, he became a warrior. In his first battle, the Indians nearly wiped out the army. The Battle of White Bird Canyon was one of the army's worst defeats.

The Nez Percé war continued into the fall. Over a four-month period, the Indians retreated nearly 1,700 miles. They fought 18 more battles and won all of them.

The Nez Percé retreat was one of the most skillful in history. With a few sharpshooters to guard the rear, the Indians held off the army.

The Indians were always outnumbered, often eight to one. And with the 150 warriors were 400 women and children, plus huge herds of cattle and horses. Yet they moved with great speed and kept ahead of their attackers.

The Indians crossed Yellowstone Park. In July, they came to the Bitterroot Mountains. Mothers and babies, little children, and old men and women climbed the narrow trail over Lolo Pass. Cattle and horses went, too. One false step meant certain death thousands of feet below.

The people of Missoula, Montana, were afraid of the approaching Indians. They set up a barricade near the end of the trail. Several hundred people blocked the way. When the Indians saw the people, they stopped. Joseph did not want to fight civilians.

During the night, Joseph took the Indians back the way they had come. They went up the side of a high cliff. Then they went down another way into the valley. They left the army struggling far behind.

The Indians moved peacefully through the valley. The settlers saw that the Indians meant them no harm. So, they sold them supplies and traded cattle and horses. The Indians kept on the run for two more months. They crossed most of Montana. Joseph had decided to go to Canada to join Sitting Bull.

By now, many of the tribe were near death. Hunger and exhaustion had taken their toll. The Indians stopped to rest near the Bear Paws Mountains. They had covered nearly 1,700 miles. They were only 40 miles from Canada and freedom. But they did not know that.

Fresh troops commanded by General Nelson Miles attacked on September 30. At the same time, a blizzard began to rage. The battle went on for five days. Both sides suffered heavy losses. Joseph soon realized that his side could not win.

On October 5, 1887, Joseph surrendered. He said:

> *I am tired of fighting. Our chiefs are killed. It is cold and we have no blankets. The little children are freezing to death. My people, some of them, have run away to the hills and have no blankets, no food. No one knows where they are, perhaps freezing to death. I want time to look for my children and see how many I can find. Maybe I shall find them among the dead. Hear me, my chiefs: I am tired; my heart is sick and sad. From where the sun now stands, I will fight no more forever.*

Miles and Joseph agreed that the Nez Percé would be returned to the Lapwai reservation. Instead, they were sent to Oklahoma. There, many died or grew weak.

Joseph was true to his word. Never again did he fight. But he continued to work for his people. He always hoped that one day they might be able to return to the Wallowa Valley.

In 1879, Joseph traveled to Washington, D.C. He explained his case to the president:

> *Let me be a free man—free to travel, to stop, free to work, free to trade where I choose, free to choose my own teachers, free to follow the religion of my fathers, free to think and talk and act for myself, and I will obey every law, or submit to the penalty.*

General Howard supported Joseph's efforts. Finally, in 1885, the Nez Percé were allowed to return to the Northwest. Part of the tribe went to the Lapwai reservation. Joseph and 150 others went to the Colville reservation in Washington state.

Joseph was never allowed to return to the Wallowa Valley to live. He died on September 21, 1904. The doctor gave the cause of death as a broken heart.

Joseph became a legend in his own time. He also became a spokesman for all Indians. In Joseph's words:

If the white man wants to live in peace with the Indian, he can live in peace. There need be no trouble. Whenever the white man treats Indians as they treat each other, then we shall have no more wars. We shall be all alike—brothers of one father and one mother, with one sky above us and one country around us, and one government for all. Then the Great Spirit Chief who rules above will smile upon this land. For this time the Indian race is waiting and praying.

Remembering the Facts

1. Why were the Nez Percé incorrectly named?

2. Why did many Nez Percé chiefs refuse to sign what they called the Thief Treaty?

3. What did Old Joseph, on his deathbed, ask of Joseph?

4. General Howard agreed the Wallowa Valley belonged to the Nez Percé. Why did he try to force the Indians to move?

5. Why was the retreat of the Nez Percé a skilled one?

6. Why was the journey over Lolo Pass amazing?

7. Why did Joseph surrender at the battle near the Bear Paws Mountains?

8. How did Joseph continue to work for his people after their surrender?

Understanding the Story

9. Why do you think the doctor gave the cause of Joseph's death as "a broken heart"?

10. At Joseph's funeral, his nephew Yellow Wolf said, "Joseph is dead, but his words are not dead. His words will live forever." What eternal truths do you think can be found in the words of Joseph? In what ways are his words like those of Martin Luther King, Jr., another fighter for freedom?

Getting the Main Idea

Joseph became a symbol of Indian resistance. During the 17 weeks that he led his people across the country, he gained the sympathy and admiration of people all over the United States. Why do you think this was true?

Applying What You Have Learned

In 1900, Joseph was allowed to visit the Wallowa Valley for the first time in the 20 years since his retreat. Write a paragraph from his point of view. Tell the changes you see. Explain your feelings upon seeing your homeland once again and knowing you will never be allowed to live there.

Sarah Winnemucca
Paiute Indian Rights Activist

An army scout. An interpreter who spoke five languages. A lecturer. A teacher. The first Indian woman to publish a book. Founder of the first Indian school. Sarah Winnemucca, a Paiute Indian, filled all these roles.

Winnemucca was a woman who was a leader. She was loved by whites throughout the country as Princess Sarah. She worked all her life for fair treatment for her people.

Winnemucca was born about 1844. Her tribe lived near Pyramid Lake in northern Nevada. It was a

Sarah Winnemucca

peaceful time. Few white settlers had seen the area. Just a few trappers and explorers had come.

She was the fourth child of Chief Winnemucca and his wife Tuboitonie. Her Indian name was Thocmetony, which means "shell flower." She later chose the name Sarah.

Winnemucca's grandfather was a leader of the tribe. He was known as Truckee. Truckee guided Captain John C. Frémont across the Sierra Nevada Mountains to California. Truckee and Frémont became close friends.

In California, Truckee learned about white people. He liked their houses and clothing. He admired the way they could write. He hoped that his people would be friends with their "white brothers."

But many Paiutes, including Winnemucca, were afraid of whites. They had heard about a group (the Donner party) who lived through a winter in the mountains by eating their dead. That meant they were cannibals.

One day, some white people neared the Paiute camp. The Indian women took their own children and ran. It was hard to run fast carrying little children. So the women hid the children, They buried them—all but their faces. Then they piled bushes over their faces. And they told them not to cry out. All day, the children lay buried. At nightfall, their mothers returned for them.

Winnemucca was one of the children. It was something she never forgot. Later she wrote: "Oh, can anyone imagine my feelings? Buried alive, thinking every minute that I was to be unburied and eaten up." It was many years before she lost her fear of white people.

When Winnemucca was six, Truckee took her, her mother, and 50 other Paiutes to visit California. Truckee carried with him a letter from Frémont. He called this paper his "rag friend." With this magic paper, he got good treatment and food from settlers.

On the trip, Winnemucca fell ill from poison oak. A white woman nursed her back to health. After that, Winnemucca lost much of her fear of whites.

Winnemucca had a gift for learning languages. While in California, she picked up English, Spanish, and several Indian languages. A white woman taught her to read, write, and sew.

After the California trip, Winnemucca returned to Nevada. While she had been away, her father was named a tribal leader. Times were getting hard. More white settlers were arriving. Winnemucca's father tried to work things out between his people and the whites.

But problems increased. These built up to the Paiute War of 1860. Finally a truce was declared. The Indians were forced to move to the Paiute reservation at Pyramid Lake, Nevada. From then on, they suffered.

Indian agents were picked to run the reservation. Many of these men were dishonest. They stole supplies sent by the government for the Indians. Then they sold the supplies and kept the money. They did little to help the Indians adjust to reservation life.

The Paiutes were now very poor. They were starving. They had little clothing. At last, they fled to the army post at Camp McDermit. There, they got food and clothing.

Winnemucca interpretered for her father as he dealt with Indian agents and army officers. She disliked the agents. She blamed them for her people's troubles. Yet she tried to keep the peace. She knew that the Indians would lose if there were a fight. She gained the respect of the settlers, the army, and her people.

In June 1868, a neighboring tribe of Bannocks went on the warpath. They were starving and had no way to support themselves. The Bannocks forced Winnemucca's father and others to join them. They held the Paiutes captive and used them as slaves.

Winnemucca knew that the army was about to attack the Bannocks. She pleaded to be allowed to rescue her father before the attack. None of the men would agree to go the Bannock camp with her.

So Winnemucca set out by herself. She followed the Bannocks' trail through Idaho and into Oregon. She traveled for three says with no sleep and little food. She arrived at the camp at night.

The Paiutes were being held in the center of camp. Winnemucca crept in. She told the women to pretend to look for firewood. Once outside the camp, the women fled. The Paiute men gave them a good head start. Then they followed. They were chased by the Bannocks. But they were able to get away.

Winnemucca gave the army information about the Bannocks. Soon afterward, the army defeated the Bannocks. Winnemucca later said, "It was the hardest work I ever did for the army."

She was not rewarded for her hard work. Instead, the government ordered the Paiutes and their enemies, the Bannocks, to the same reservation. The reservation was in Yakima, Washington, 350 miles away. It was winter.

The Indians had little food or warm clothing. Many people died during the trip, which took months. When the Indians arrived in Yakima, the agent was not expecting them. There was no shelter. There were no supplies. Hastily, a large shed was built. There, over 500 Paiutes were housed.

Over the years, things did not improve much. Winnemucca sent messages to anyone who might be able to help. She traveled to San Francisco. There, she gave lectures on the problems of the Indians. Her lectures were very popular. She became known as Princess Sarah.

In 1879, Winnemucca was invited to lecture in Washington, D.C. She met President Rutherford Hayes and his secretary of the interior. They promised help. But their promises were never kept.

In 1883, Winnemucca wrote the story of the Paiutes. Her book was called *Life Among the Paiutes: Their Wrongs and Claims.* This was the first book written by a Native American woman.

In 1884, Winnemucca founded the Peabody School, near Lovelock, Nevada. It was to be a model school for Indian children. The children were taught English as well as their own language and culture. Four years later, the school ran out of funds and had to close.

Winnemucca's health failed in her last few years. In 1891, she died, probably from tuberculosis. She was 47 years old.

She died thinking that she had failed her people. But she was not a failure. Her writings and lectures made people aware of the Indian's problems. Her book tells the history of her people. She is remembered as someone who never gave up the fight for her people.

A marker on the McDermit Indian reservation in Nevada honors Winnemucca. It states: "She was a believer in the brotherhood of mankind."

Remembering the Facts

1. Name three roles that Winnemucca played in her fight for her people.

   (a)

   (b)

   (c)

2. Where did the Paiute tribe live?

3. How did Truckee learn about the white man's ways?

4. Why did the Indians think that Truckee's "rag friend" was magic?

5. Why did Winnemucca dislike most of the Indian agents?

6. Name two ways that Winnemucca told the nation about the problems of the Paiutes.

7. Why was the Peabody School forced to close?

8. Why did Winnemucca die thinking that she was a failure?

Understanding the Story

9. The Peabody School was to be a model school for Indian education. How do you think that its ideas would be accepted by Native American educators today? Why?

10. Why do you think that so many Indian agents treated the Indians badly? Why do you think that they got away with this?

Getting the Main Idea

Why do you think that Sarah Winnemucca is remembered as one of the great Native American women of all time?

Applying What You've Learned

Winnemucca spoke to many groups on the East Coast about the troubles of the Paiutes. What things do you think she might talk about to gain the support of her white audiences?

Ishi
Yahi Survivor and Research Assistant

The foothills of Mount Lassen, in northern California, were rugged. They were covered with a dense brush called *chaparral*. The brush was often so thick that a person had to cut his way through it. Higher up, the hills were bare rocks. A series of ridges were framed by deep canyons. Above all this stood Mount Lassen, an ancient volcano.

It was a hard place to live. But it was full of good places to hide. Trails under the chaparral were hidden. The steep canyon walls made it hard to see the floor below. Rocks, trees, and caves provided more hiding places.

Ishi

Hiding was a matter of life or death for the Yana Indians who lived there. Even the little children knew that they must never be seen or heard by anyone from the outside. Once seen, they were certain to be killed.

It was not always this way. For 3,000 to 4,000 years, the Yana lived peacefully in the Sacramento Valley. The tribe was small— 2,000 to 3,000 people. It was split into four groups. These groups lived apart, gathering only once a year.

Nearly 1,000 years ago, a stronger tribe invaded the valley. The Yana were pushed up into the foothills. There, they were left alone. Adapting to their new land, they went about their lives.

In 1848, gold was discovered in the hills. Thousands of people came looking for gold. Many who did not find gold settled in the valley. The Yana were cut off from their fishing streams and hunting grounds. They were hungry most of the time.

The Yana fought back. But the more they did, the more the whites wanted to kill them. By 1872, the whites thought that all the Yana had been killed.

They were wrong. A dozen Yana were still hiding in the foothills. They were members of the Yahi group of Yanas. Into this small group Ishi was born around 1862. By the time the boy was 10, only a handful of Yahi were left.

The Yahi hid during the day. At night they came out, looking for food. They could make no sound. They could leave no footprints. Over the years, the Yahi died one by one.

The last four Yahi hid in a place they called Grizzly Bear's Hiding Place. They were Ishi, his sick mother, his sister, and a man.

Still, they faithfully followed the customs and religion of their people. Even their tools and weapons were like those used in the Stone Age.

In November 1908, the Yahi heard men approaching the hiding place. The three healthy Yahi ran outside and hid. There was no time to move Ishi's sick mother. She was inside, wrapped in a blanket. The men did not bother the dying woman. But they took the Indians' tools and supplies for souvenirs.

The man and Ishi's sister tried to escape down a nearby river. They probably drowned. When the men left, Ishi came back and moved his mother. She died a few days later. Ishi was totally alone.

For three years, Ishi wandered the hills. He spent winters in a cave. He was always hungry. He was always afraid he would be found.

In August 1911, Ishi left the foothills. He was starving. And he was lonely. He had lived nearly 50 years in the wilderness. He walked 40 miles to the town of Oroville.

Just outside town, he collapsed. A pack of dogs attacked him. A white man drove the dogs off. The man couldn't believe his eyes.

Ishi looked like a wild man. His clothing was dirty and torn. He was so thin that his bones showed through his skin. His hair was matted and burned off close to his head.

Ishi was sure that he would be killed. But the sheriff arrived. For lack of a better idea, he put Ishi in jail. He gave him food. The starving man ate it all hungrily. People tried to talk to Ishi in different languages. But he understood no one.

Ishi's story hit the newspapers fast. He was called the Wild Man of Oroville. Ishi was a real mystery. Where had he come from? Were there more like him?

Professors Thomas Waterman and Alfred Kroeber heard about Ishi. They studied Indians at the University of California in Berkeley. They thought Ishi might be a Yana.

Waterman came to Oroville with a list of Yana words. Ishi was thrilled to hear someone speak his language. The two men became friends. Waterman took Ishi to San Francisco. The Stone Age man entered the twentieth century.

Ishi's new home was a room in the Museum of Anthropology at the University of California. At first, he was afraid of the many noises around him. But he was treated kindly. And he quickly learned not to be afraid.

Kroeber became Ishi's second friend. He gave Ishi his name. The Yana never revealed their true name to anyone. So Kroeber chose the name Ishi, meaning "man" in Yana.

Some people wanted to use Ishi. Circuses, sideshows, and movie companies wanted to make money by putting Ishi on display. Kroeber said no. He wanted Ishi to live as normal a life as possible.

Ishi was a calm and gentle person. He was interested in everything around him. He loved modern ways. He was thrilled by doorknobs, telephones, and typewriters. Matches and window shades were a real puzzle. He found that glue was most useful. Ishi learned quickly about his new home.

People wanted to learn about Ishi, too. Two months after Ishi arrived, the museum opened to the public. Thousands of visitors came to see Ishi on Sunday afternoons. Soon, he got used to the attention. He proudly showed visitors how to string a bow or make an arrowhead.

During the week, Ishi taught the professors more about his language and culture. He also worked as an assistant janitor for the museum. He earned $25 a month. He liked doing his own shopping. He enjoyed fixing meals in the museum kitchen. He traveled around San Francisco on his own. He adopted his new world. He felt at home.

In the spring of 1914, Ishi's friends planned a trip back to visit Ishi's old home. Ishi showed them where the Yahi had lived.

He showed them the ways the Yahi hunted and fished. He lured animals to him by making special sounds. He pointed out different plants and explained their uses.

Waterman and Kroeber recorded this information about Yahi life. They took photographs of Ishi as he showed how to make tools and weapons. They also took photos of him hunting and fishing. A good picture of the Yahi way of life began to take shape.

A month later, the group returned to San Francisco. Ishi happily took up his work in the museum. But soon he fell ill with tuberculosis. He died on March 25, 1916.

Nearly 50 years later, Kroeber's wife, Theodora Kroeber, wrote Ishi's biography. The book was a best-seller. Interest in Ishi's life grew. In 1984, the Ishi Wilderness was set aside in the Lassen National Forest. In 1966, a historical marker was erected near Oroville. It read:

The Last Yahi Indian

For thousands of years, the Yahi Indians roamed the foothills between Mount Lassen and the Sacramento Valley. Settlement of this region by the white man brought death to the Yahi by gun, by disease, and by hunger. By the turn of the century, only a few remained. Ishi, the last known survivor of these people, was discovered at this site in 1911. His death in 1916 brought an end to Stone Age California.

Remembering the Facts

1. Why were the Yahi Indians able to go so long without being found?

2. Why did the Yahi and the whites first come into conflict?

3. How did the Yahi follow the ancient ways of their people?

4. Why were so many people interested in Ishi when he was found?

5. How did Professor Waterman make Ishi feel at ease when they first met?

6. Where did Ishi live in San Francisco?

7. Why did Ishi work as a janitor?

8. What did Ishi do on Sunday afternoons?

9. What things did Ishi like about in his new home?

10. How did Ishi die?

Understanding the Story

11.   Why were the anthropologists at the museum so eager to study Ishi?

12.   Why is Ishi's story one of both tragedy and triumph?

Getting the Main Idea

Why is the story of Ishi important in the story of America?

Applying What You've Learned

Imagine that you are a young Yahi Indian living at the time of Ishi. Describe your daily life. What are your thoughts? How do you find the courage to continue such a difficult life? How does it feel to live on fear of discovery and sudden death?

Susan LaFlesche Picotte
Omaha Physician

Susan LaFlesche Picotte was born June 17, 1865, on the Omaha reservation in Nebraska. Her mother was part Iowa Indian. Her father was the son of a French fur trader and an Osage woman. Known as Iron Eye, he was chief of the Omahas.

The years after the Civil War were a time of rapid change for the Omahas. They had already given up their lands to the whites. The buffalo were gone. White men had moved in all around them. The Omahas were under the control of the U.S. government.

Susan LaFlesche Picotte

Iron Eye was a good leader for these times. As a young man, he traveled widely with his father. He saw the cities of the East Coast. He saw the changes around him. He believed that to survive, the Indian had to adapt to the white world.

He raised his five children to know both Indian and white ways. The children all adopted some white ways. They also spent much of their lives fighting for the rights of their people. All went on to do great work in their fields.

One was a noted speaker on Indian rights. One was a businesswoman. Another taught at the Indian school. Another was an anthropologist who wrote many books about the Omahas. And Susan LaFlesche Picotte became the first Native American woman doctor.

When their first child was born, the LaFlesche family lived in an earthen lodge. When the fifth one was born, they lived in a modern frame house. The children grew up speaking their native tongue.

Picotte went to the mission school on the reservation. There, she learned to speak English. When she was 14, she was sent to the Elizabeth Institute for three years. This was a finishing school in New Jersey. There, she learned the social graces, plus art and music.

Picotte went on to the Hampton Institute in Virginia. This was one of the first government colleges for Indians. She graduated in 1886. She got a gold medal for high grades.

She had strong religious beliefs. She joined the Women's National Indian Association. This was a Christian women's group. Its goal was to train native missionaries. These missionaries taught the Indians Christian values.

The association agreed to pay for Picotte's medical schooling. In return, she agreed to be a medical missionary to the Omahas.

Picotte studied at the Women's Medical College in Philadelphia. She graduated in 1889 at the head of her class. She became the first Native American woman doctor.

She spoke to many groups about the needs of her people. She was well liked in the town. She was a guest at the finest homes.

After graduation, Picotte could have taken up private practice at the Women's Hospital. Her life would have been one of comfort and luxury.

But she wanted to return to the reservation. She won a government job as doctor for the Omahas.

The job was hard. The reservation was huge. The 1,300 Indians were scattered all over it. There were few roads. Picotte rode on horseback to reach those who needed her. She answered calls day and night, in all kinds of weather. She rode in subzero weather through drifts of snow. She never turned down anyone who asked for help.

Travel was so slow, she often arrived late. But the people were glad to see her. Picotte offered them her comfort. They gladly shared the little food they had.

Not everyone liked her work. Many older Indians did not trust "the white man's medicine." Picotte had to convince them to let her help them.

No one helped her in her work. There was no other doctor or nurse. There was no hospital on the reservation. But Picotte continued this hard work for five years. Then her health gave out. She was forced to rest for a while.

In 1894, she married a man who was half Sioux and half French. The couple settled in the town of Bancroft, Nebraska. They had two boys. Then Picotte took up medicine again. Over her 25 years of practice, she treated almost every member of the Omaha tribe. She also treated many whites.

In 1905, her husband died. Picotte became a missionary to the Omahas. A year later, the town of Walthill was founded nearby. Picotte went to live there. She was one of the town's leading citizens.

She started the county medical society. She lobbied the government for public health laws. In 1913, she achieved a lifelong goal. She opened a hospital for the Omahas in Walthill.

One major health problem for many Indians was alcoholism. Picotte fought against the sale of liquor on the reservation. As she wrote in 1914, "Men, women, and children drank. Men and women died from alcoholism. Little children were seen reeling on the streets of the town. Drunken brawls in which men were killed occurred. No person's life was safe."

Picotte headed a group that went to Washington, D.C. They wanted to outlaw liquor sales on the reservation. She succeeded in getting liquor sales banned in Walthill. Many of the Omahas were angry about this. But no one could deny that alcohol was a big problem.

Another issue that Picotte fought for was the right for the Omahas to own land. The government held the reservation land in trust for the Indians. The Indians were not allowed to own land. They resented this policy. Picotte and her older sister asked the secretary of the interior for help. Finally, a new law was passed. The Omahas could own land on the reservation.

As Picotte neared the age of 50, her health failed. On September 18, 1916, she died in the Walthill hospital that she had founded. The hospital was later renamed in her honor.

Picotte was the first Native American woman doctor. But she is remembered for much more. She was important in the Indian rights movement. She was involved in the women's movement, as well.

As an Indian activist, Picotte was ahead of her time. She worked for her own tribe and for Native Americans nationwide. At a time when women were not usually in charge, Susan LaFlesche Picotte was respected as a leader of her people.

Remembering the Details

1. Why did Iron Eye see the changes that were about to happen to the Omahas?

2. Why did Iron Eye teach his children white ways?

3. Where did Picotte attend medical school?

4. Why did the Indian Association pay for Picotte's schooling?

5. Why did Picotte return to the reservation?

6. Name three reasons the reservation job was difficult.

7. What lifelong goal did Picotte reach in Walthill?

8. Why did Picotte work to have the sale of liquor outlawed in Walthill?

9. Why couldn't Indians own land on the reservation?

30428

Understanding the Story

10. Why do you think that so few Native American women were in positions of leadership during the ninteenth century?

11. Why do you think that alcoholism became such a problem on the reservations?

Getting the Main Idea

Why do you think Picotte is an outstanding role model for young women today?

Applying What You've Learned

Imagine that you are an Indian teenager living on a reservation in the early 1900's. Your family is poor. The adults are unemployed alcoholics. Write a paragraph telling why the pull of alcohol might be strong on you. Then tell what factors could help you stay away from it.

ORLAND PARK PUBLIC LIBRARY

Jim Thorpe
Sauk and Fox Athlete

If asked to name the greatest athlete who ever lived, many people might think of one of today's highly paid athletes. Many might not remember Jim Thorpe. But he was an amazing athlete whose story should not be forgotten.

Jim Thorpe

Thorpe was born on May 22, 1887, in a one-room cabin in Oklahoma. He had a twin brother named Charles. His mother was a Potawatomi Indian. His father was half Irish and half Sauk and Fox Indian. Thorpe's mother was a descendant of the Sauk and Fox chief Black Hawk.

Black Hawk was a famous warrior. He was an outstanding athlete as well. He was both strong and fast. Thorpe's mother believed that her son was the great chief reborn.

The Thorpe twins spent most of their time outside. They loved riding horses, hunting, swimming, and fishing. They played athletic games, one after the other.

This way of life led to Thorpe's later success in athletics. He had no coach, no team, and no organized practice. He learned endurance, quickness, and agility from all his outside work and play.

When Thorpe was six, his carefree life ended. His father sent the twins to the Sauk and Fox Mission School. The school was 25 miles from home. So the boys lived at the school.

The goal of the school was to break the Indian children of being Indians. This way they could learn to fit into the white man's world. To do this, the school had strict rules. The children had to wear dark suits and black felt hats. They were forbidden to speak their Indian languages. Their time was planned from early morning until late at night.

Thorpe hated everything about the school—except for one thing: baseball. He lived for the afternoons when the boys played ball.

The twins were nine years old when Charles died. Thorpe was very lonely for his twin. Without him, he could not stand being at school. He ran away again and again.

The following fall, Thorpe's father sent him to Haskell Institute. Haskell was a military school in Kansas. It had a strict program of classes, manual labor, and discipline. Thorpe's father hoped the program would help his son pull himself together.

At Haskell, Thorpe first heard about football. He and his friends spent hours playing with a homemade football. Thorpe also enjoyed running track.

In 1904, Thorpe went to the Carlisle Industrial Indian School in Pennsylvania. He liked its sports program. One day, he saw high jumpers trying to clear a bar set at 5'9". None of them could make it. Thorpe, dressed in overalls, asked if he could try. The team laughed. But Thorpe cleared the bar easily. The next day, Thorpe was a member of the varsity squad. That season, he broke every Carlisle record in track and field.

Thorpe was good at every sport he tried. He lettered in 11 sports: football, track, lacrosse, baseball, gymnastics, hockey, boxing, wrestling, swimming, handball, and basketball.

In 1909, Thorpe played baseball on a semipro team during the summer. He was paid $2 a day for expenses. But he wasn't in it for the money. Thorpe just loved to play baseball. Four years later, that summer of semipro ball cost him dearly.

Thorpe soon came to the attention of Carlisle football coach Glenn "Pop" Warner. Warner asked Thorpe to try out for the team.

On his first day, Thorpe carried the ball and dodged his way through the whole team. He scored a touchdown without anyone touching him. Thorpe was a natural!

He also had a great coach. Warner drove his players hard. It paid off. The Carlisle Indians beat all of the major college football teams.

Thorpe scored most of the points by himself. He was good at everything: running, passing, and kicking. He punted the ball so high and ran so fast he could beat the ball down the field. He kicked a punt of 83 yards. Thorpe was nearly the whole team by himself.

As Warner said, "Jim Thorpe knew everything a football player could be taught. He could make a play work better than the coach ever dreamed." Thorpe was voted All-American Halfback in 1911 and 1912.

But more was to come. In the 1912 Carlisle track and field season, Thorpe won every meet for the school—by himself. That year, he qualified for the U.S. Olympic Track Team.

At the Olympics, Thorpe was stunning. He won the gold medal for the five-event pentathlon. He won the 200-meter dash, broad jump, 1500-meter run, and discus throw. In the javelin throw, he came in third. To this day, Thorpe's record has not been equaled.

But Thorpe was not done. The decathlon was next. In those days, athletes competed in 10 different events over a three-day period. The events included the 100-meter dash, 400-meter race, 1500-meter race, the javelin and discus throws, the shot put, the high jump, the long jump, a hurdle race, and the pole vault. Again, Thorpe won the gold medal. His Olympic record in the decathlon stood for many years.

King Gustav of Sweden presented the Olympic medals. When he shook Thorpe's hand, he said, "Sir, you are the greatest athlete in the world." Thorpe did not know what to say. He answered, "Thanks, King." It was the proudest moment of Thorpe's life.

Thorpe's glory lasted only six months. A reporter learned that Thorpe had been paid for playing baseball. The Amateur Athletic Union said that that made him a pro. As a pro, he had not been eligible for the Olympics. Thorpe was stripped of his medals. His name was removed from the record books.

The loss of his medals upset Thorpe greatly. But he did not fight the Amateur Athletic Union. He had never tried to hide his baseball "career." He had not known that being a paid player made him ineligible.

Sports fans everywhere were outraged. Some argued that Thorpe was a pro in baseball, but not in track. Other fans named athletes who had done the same as Thorpe. They felt that Thorpe had been treated unfairly. Still, the ruling stood.

Thorpe's life had its share of tragedies: the loss of his twin brother, being orphaned at 16, the death of his two-year-old son, and two divorces. Through it all, Thorpe kept going.

In 1913, Thorpe signed with the New York Giants baseball team. He played baseball 15 more years, until he was 40. During the same years, he played pro football. From 1915 to 1920, he played with the Canton, Ohio, Bulldogs. In 1921, he played with the Cleveland Indians. Then in 1922, he formed his own all-Indian football team. The team was called Jim Thorpe's Oorang Indians.

Thorpe went on to play for six other teams. His last football game was for the Chicago Cardinals in 1929. He was 41 years old.

When Thorpe retired from sports, he worked at a variety of jobs. Money was always scarce. He got bit parts in movies. He worked as a referee for dance marathons. He painted gas stations and trucks. He worked digging ditches for 50 cents an hour.

When the 1932 Olympics came to Los Angeles, Thorpe could not afford a ticket. The vice president of the United States, Charles Curtis (an American Indian himself), asked Thorpe to sit with him. The fans gave Thorpe a standing ovation. To them, he was still a hero.

Thorpe traveled to schools to speak to young people. He never asked for pay. His message was clear: "Athletics gives you a fighting spirit to battle your problems in life. Athletics builds sportsmanship."

Thorpe supported Native American issues. He toured the country, giving speeches. He talked about his sports and about Indian traditions. He hoped to raise money to help improve Indian living conditions.

In 1949, Thorpe's life story was made into a movie. It was called *Jim Thorpe—All American.* Thorpe was played by Burt Lancaster.

In 1950, more honors came to Thorpe. An Associated Press poll voted him the greatest male athlete of the first half of the twentieth century. He was also named the greatest American football player for the same period.

On March 28, 1953, Thorpe died of a heart attack. He was buried in Pennsylvania, not far from the Carlisle Indian School. Two small towns, Mauch Chunk and East Mauch Chunk, merged and took the name Jim Thorpe. The new town built a monument to honor the world's greatest athlete.

Several groups asked the Olympic Committee to restore Thorpe's medals. Nearly 30 years later, in 1982, an Olympic committee finally restored Thorpe's amateur status. His medals and his place in the record books were returned to his family. Thorpe had married three times and had eight children.

Jim Thorpe's talents brought him great fame. But they also brought a lifetime of problems. They never brought him wealth or happiness. But through all the difficulties of his life, Thorpe remained a humble and cheerful man.

Thorpe often told his children, "A good person is better than a great athlete." King Gustav of Sweden was right. Jim Thorpe was the world's greatest athlete. And he was a first-rate person as well.

Remembering the Details

1. To what famous warrior was Thorpe related?

2. How did the Indian schools try to take away the Indian children's culture?

3. Name three sports Thorpe excelled in at Carlisle.

4. Who was the football coach at Carlisle?

5. What did Thorpe do as a student that later cost him his Olympic gold medals?

6. For what two events did Thorpe win gold medals?

7. What two professional sports did Thorpe play after the Olympics?

8. What honors came to Thorpe in 1950?

Understanding the Story

9. Thorpe's Indian name was Wa-Tho-Hack, which means "Bright Path." Many times, Thorpe said he was not sure that he had been well named. In what ways do you think Thorpe's life was a bright path or a dark path?

10. There are many great stars in pro sports today. In what ways is Thorpe different from all the rest?

Getting the Main Idea

Why do you think Thorpe is a good role model for young athletes of today?

Applying What You've Learned

Imagine you are a sports fan living in 1912. Write a letter to the Amateur Athletic Union tell how you feel about their taking Thorpe's gold medals.

Maria Martinez
Pueblo Potter

San Ildefonso is a tiny village, 20 miles northwest of Santa Fe, New Mexico. It was settled nearly 700 years ago by the Pueblo Indians.

Over the years, San Ildefonso has been home to as few as 80 people. In good times, the population has been as high as 400. Disease and drought have kept numbers small. During the sixteenth century, the Spanish killed many of the villagers. And the infant death rate has always been high.

Over the years, the people of San Ildefonso kept to themselves. They

Maria Martinez

held fast to their traditional way of life. Farming was the main work. But the land was not rich. And there was little rain. The people were very poor.

During the twentieth century, San Ildefonso has seen change. Today, the village is home to a group of successful artists. This has happened mainly because of one woman: Maria Montoya Martinez.

Martinez has been called the most famous Indian artist of all time. Together with her husband, she brought back the ancient art of pottery making. The couple turned a simple craft into a beautiful art form. In doing so, they brought prosperity to their village.

Martinez was born about 1881 in San Ildefonso. Her family lived in the old ways. Her father was a farmer. Her mother took care of the house and the children. Her aunt, Nicolasa Montoya, made fine pots. It was from her aunt that Martinez learned pottery making.

Martinez and her two sisters went to day school in the village. Later, the Pueblo council sent Martinez to St. Catherine's mission school in Santa Fe. It was a great honor to be chosen. After two years, she had finished her schooling. It was not proper for a Pueblo girl to have more education than this.

At St. Catherine's, Martinez met her future husband. He was also from San Ildefonso. But he was different from most village men. He hated farming. For this reason, some of the Indians looked down on him.

The couple were well matched. Both were artistic. They tried to do perfect work. Both were creative in their thinking. Together, they revolutionized pottery making.

The couple were married in 1904. They spent their honeymoon at the St. Louis World's Fair. They had been hired to show the Pueblo lifestyle to visitors at the fair.

At the fair, Martinez made some simple pots. Her husband painted them. The couple sold many pots. But the pots brought little money. The couple returned home. Their first two children were born.

The Pueblo people had made pottery for centuries. But the art had declined over the years. Few women made pots. If they did, they were plain pots for kitchen use. Most of the ancient techniques had been lost.

Near the village were ruins of ancient cliff dwellings. In 1907, a group of archaeologists came to the area. They wanted to explore the sites. A whole buried city was found. Pieces of pottery and other objects appeared. Paintings were found on the walls of a cave.

Martinez's husband was hired to help dig at the ruins. He found the work interesting. He carefully dug and sifted the earth, looking for old objects. He began copying the designs from the objects. The scientists saw his skill. They asked hime to do more drawings. He enjoyed using his talent in this way.

One scientist was director of the Museum of New Mexico in Santa Fe. He wanted to have ancient pots re-created. He brought a small piece (called a potsherd) of an unusual pot to Martinez. He asked if a whole pot could be made, using the piece as a guide. Martinez agreed to try.

During the winter of 1908, Martinez and her husband worked on the pot. They experimented with different sands and clays. They made paintbrushes from yucca leaves, as the ancients had done. They practiced the designs. The scientists were pleased with their work and paid them well.

The pair were very talented. Martinez made perfectly shaped pots without the use of a potter's wheel. Her husband never measured before he drew. But his designs always came out right.

In 1911, the museum director asked the couple to live at the museum. The two lived there for three years. They showed visitors how they made their pottery. And they sold the pots to the public. They also studied the ancient pottery on display. They made money doing something they loved.

One day, a mistake produced pots that were all black. This happened when the fire was accidentally smothered. The normally reddish pottery was chemically changed to a shiny black. This process had been known in ancient times. By accident, the couple had rediscovered it.

The black pottery was pretty. But the designs painted on it would not stay. In 1919, the finally couple came up with a black-on-black technique. They etched the design onto the shiny black pot in a flat black. This technique brought the couple fame and fortune.

The first of these pots were sold for a few dollars. Before long, they were selling for thousands of dollars. Today, they are collector's items found in fine museums.

Martinez was becoming famous. But, following Indian tradition, she did not wish to be better than the other village members. So, she began teaching men and women the techniques. This was a change. Before, pottery making had been only for women. Soon, thanks to Martinez, many villagers were making a good living from their pottery.

Her husband died in 1943. Martinez carried on their work. In 1956, her son, Popovi Da, became her new partner. The two continued the tradition.

Martinez died in 1980 at the age of 98. But the effect of her work lives on. Many members of her village make and sell pottery today. Grandchildren, great-grandchildren, and great-great grandchildren carry on the family art. A museum in San Ildefonso details the lifework of Martinez.

A "Maria pot" today sells for many thousands of dollars. She has left behind many elegant works of art. But her true legacy is in the generations of artists she inspired.

Martinez received many awards for her work. But the one that meant the most to her was the title Mother of the Pueblo. She was given this title by the grateful people of San Ildefonso.

Indeed, she deserved the title. For where there once was a struggling group of farmers near starvation, there is now a group of families who are running a successful business.

In 1968, Martinez told a reporter from the *Albuquerque Journal:*

> *Among my own great-grandchildren, some have gone into nursing and electronics, and I am happy they have. Others are staying in the [village] and have an interest in the old ways and crafts. And I am happy they are. There is a place for both the old and the new, and they will find their places.*

Remembering the Facts

1. Where is the village of San Ildefonso?

2. Give two reasons why the village population is small.

    (a)   (b)

3. What work did most Pueblo men do?

4. How did Martinez learn to make pots?

5. How were the ancient potsherds found?

6. In what ways did their work at the museum help Martinez and her husband develop their art?

7. Describe the pots for which Martinez became famous.

8. How did pottery making transform the San Ildefonso?

Understanding the Story

9. Why do you think Martinez earned of her title Mother of the Pueblo?

10. Why do you think ancient art forms might be lost over time?

Getting the Main Idea

Why do you think Martinez had such an important influence in the life of Native Americans throughout the Southwest?

Applying What You've Learned

Sketch and explain a design for a container to be made from materials native to your area. The container should be able to hold liquids. It should be decorated with symbols that are meaningful to you.

Annie Dodge Wauneka
Navajo Health Educator

The Presidential Medal of Freedom is the highest civilian honor a person can get. Only a few outstanding Americans have won this award.

In 1964, President Lyndon B. Johnson presented the first of these awards. He called the name of Annie Dodge Wauneka. A six-foot-tall Native American woman stepped forward. She wore traditional Navajo clothing: a long printed skirt, a velveteen blouse, and silver and turquoise jewelry.

Wauneka was the first Native American to receive this award. Her award read:

Annie Dodge Wauneka

> *First woman elected to the Navajo Tribal Council. By her long crusade for improved health programs, she has helped dramatically to lessen the menace of disease among her people and to improve their way of life.*

Wauneka always wore the medal pinned to her blouse. So the Navajos call her the Badge Woman.

Wauneka was born on April 10, 1910, in a hogan near Sawmill, Arizona. A hogan is a small, round building made of logs. It has no windows. It has a dirt floor. In the center is a fire spot with a smoke hole in the roof. The hogan is the Navajo home.

Wauneka's father was a wealthy rancher and tribal leader. Following Navajo custom, he married two sisters. Later, he married again. The third wife was Wauneka's mother.

Wauneka's father had a large home. He had three other children by his first two wives.

The children grew up in comfort. But the father did not want them to feel they were better than other Navajos. So he made them work hard around the ranch.

From age five, Wauneka cared for the sheep. She got up at sunrise. She took the sheep out to the hills. She watched over them. She made sure none were lost. At mid-morning she returned home. She had breakfast. Then she went back to the hills for the day, carrying her lunch.

Wauneka saw that her father was an important man. Many Navajos came to him, asking for advice. The home was often full of important guests.

Navajo law said that no person was better than anyone else. All were equal. Wauneka's father had become richer than any Navajo. But he was not resented. He worked all his life to help his people.

At that time, few Navajos went to school. There were no schools nearby. And the Navajos feared going outside the tribe. But Wauneka's father sent his children to boarding schools. He wanted them to have the education that he never had.

At age eight, Wauneka went to the government school at Fort Defiance, Arizona. That year, the flu epidemic of World War I struck. Thousands of people died. Many children at the school became ill. Some died. Wauneka had a mild case of the flu and then got better.

The school had only one nurse to care for the sick children. So, Wauneka helped the nurse. She fed and cared for the sick for hours on end. This remained one of Wauneka's vivid memories. It sparked her interest in Indian health.

For sixth grade, Wauneka went to the Albuquerque Indian School in New Mexico. She was an excellent student. All classes were in English. She learned quickly. While there, she met the man she later married.

While Wauneka was away, her father became first chairman of the Navajo tribal council. When Wauneka returned to the reservation, she got married. Over the years, the couple had six children.

Theirs was not a traditional Navajo marriage. The husband tended the home and the herds. Wauneka traveled the reservation as her father's aide.

She saw parts of the reservation she did not know about. She saw many living in poverty and sickness. Wauneka wanted to do something to improve her people's health. She decided to run for the tribal council.

In 1951, she became the first woman elected to the Navajo tribal council. She was elected chairman of the health committee. Her first task: to do battle with tuberculosis. Tuberculosis was the leading cause of death among Indians. It was a difficult, uphill fight.

First, Wauneka had to learn more about tuberculosis. She spent three months in U.S. Public Health Service hospitals. She studied the causes and treatment of the disease. Then she shared her knowledge with her people.

This was not as easy as it sounds. Most Navajos feared going to a white man's hospital. They wanted to use their medicine men. There were not even any Navajo words for "germs" or "shots."

First, Wauneka visited Indian tuberculosis patients in the hospital. She explained about the "bugs that eat the body" (germs). She told them how the white man's medicine could kill the bugs.

Next, she spoke with the medicine men, one at a time. She listened to their ideas about disease. Then she talked about tuberculosis. She explained that it was a disease found all over the world. It would take both white and Indian medicine to beat it. Then she set up meetings between doctors and medicine men. She helped the two groups know and understand each other.

Wauneka also wrote a health dictionary. In it, she translated English medical and health terms into Navajo. She also explained terms for which there was no Navajo word.

Next, she worked on getting more people with tuberculosis to go to the hospital. She visited them in their hogans. She explained to them how they were spreading the disease every time they coughed. As soon as she made any progress with sick people, she took them to the hospital before they changed their mind.

In 1955, the Public Health Service began building hospitals and clinics on the reservation. Wauneka encouraged the Navajos to use these facilities. There they would get free treatment.

Wauneka thought of other ways to teach the Navajos about health. She helped make two films about good health habits. And she gave a weekly radio program. In it she talked about many health topics.

Wauneka knew the hogans caused health problems. The dirt floors could not be made clean. There were no windows to let in fresh air and light. Too many people lived too close together.

Today, most Navajos have moved out of their hogans. They now live in new homes with floors, windows, and indoor plumbing. The hogans remain nearby. They are used for ceremonies.

Tuberculosis was not the only health problem. Wauneka also worked for better prenatal care. She urged mothers to get check-ups for their babies. Wauneka's work lowered the infant death rate on the reservation.

Today alcoholism is the main killer on Indian reservations. Wauneka worked to teach her people about alcohol abuse.

In the mid-1950's, Wauneka went back to school. She earned a bachelor's degree in public health from the University of Arizona. In 1976, she received an honorary doctor of public health degree. Then, in 1996, the university awarded her an honorary doctor of law degree.

In her lifetime, Annie Dodge Wauneka earned many honors. She served on presidential committees, including the U.S. Surgeon General's Committee on Indian Health. In 1984, the Navajo Council gave her the title Legendary Mother of the Navajo People.

Wauneka inspired Native Americans of all tribes. She was able to mix the old and the new ways in her life. She was an important force in helping the Navajos and whites understand and respect each other.

Remembering the Facts

1. What important award did Wauneka receive in 1964?

2. How did Wauneka's father keep his children from feeling better than those who had less?

3. Why was Wauneka's father not resented, even though he was rich?

4. How did Wauneka become interested in Indian health?

5. Why did Wauneka want to be on the tribal council?

6. How did Wauneka learn about tuberculosis?

7. What kind of book did Wauneka write to help fight tuberculosis?

8. How did Wauneka get the medicine men to help fight tuberculosis?

9. Name two other health issues that Wauneka worked on.

10. What is the main killer on the Navajo reservation today?

Understanding the Story

11. Wauneka has been honored by the Navajo Council as the Legendary Mother of the Navajo People. Why do you think they gave her this title?

12. Why do you think tuberculosis was the leading cause of death on the reservations many years after antibiotics were developed?

Getting the Main Idea

Why do you think Wauneka was chosen to receive the Presidential Medal of Freedom?

Applying What You've Learned

Alcoholism is the leading cause of death on the Navajo reservation today. Make a list of ways you think Wauneka might have attacked this problem.

N. Scott Momaday
Kiowa Poet and Writer

In northeast Wyoming, the pine forests of the Black Hills meet the vast plains. Jutting 1,000 feet out of the earth above the Belle Fourche River is a stump-shaped rock. The rock is known as Devil's Tower. To the Indians who lived near there, it was a sacred place.

Kiowa writer N. Scott Momaday spoke of Devil's Tower in his book *House Made of Dawn:*

N. Scott Momaday

> *There are things in nature which engender an awful quiet in the heart of man. Devil's Tower is one of them. Man must account for it. He must never fail to explain such a thing to himself, or else he is estranged forever from the universe. Two centuries ago, because they could not do otherwise, the Kiowas made a legend at the base of the rock.*

The Kiowa legend explained the origin of the rock. Momaday retold the Kiowa story:

> *Eight children were there at play, seven sisters and their brother. Suddenly the boy was struck dumb. He trembled and began to run upon his hands and feet. His fingers became claws, and his body was covered with fur. There was a bear where the boy had been.*

> *The sisters were terrified. They ran, and the bear ran after them. They came to the stump of a great tree, and the tree spoke to them. It bade them climb upon it, and as they did so it began to rise into the air. The bear came to kill them, but they were just beyond its reach. It reared against the tree*

and scored the bark all around with its claws. The seven sisters were borne into the sky, and they became the stars of the Big Dipper.

In the story, the stump was Devil's Tower. The claw marks formed the ridges that run up and down the tower. And the sisters became stars in the sky.

Momaday was bornon February 27, 1934 in Lawton, Oklahoma. His father, a full-blooded Kiowa, was the artist Alfred Momaday. His mother, Mayme Natachee Scott, came from from a white pioneer family. Her great-grandmother was Cherokee.

When Momaday was six months old, his parents took him to see Devil's Tower. It is known as Tsoai or "rock tree" in Kiowa. Momaday was then given the Kiowa name of Tsoai-talee, or "Rock Tree Boy." This was a name of great honor and meaning.

To an Indian, a child's name is very important. It has meaning that will direct the course of the child's life. When Momaday was named after the sacred Devil's Tower, it was a prophecy. His life was to be of great importance to his people.

This prophecy came true. Momaday became one of the most famous Native American writers. In 1969, he became the first Native American to win the Pulitzer Prize for fiction. His impact on Native American literature has had no equal.

Momaday was an only child. He learned at an early age to use his imagination. With it, he created playmates and games for himself.

When Momaday was 12, his family moved to Jemez, New Mexico. To Momaday, the land around this mountain village was full of mystery and life. He explored endlessly on horseback. Within that landscape, he discovered himself.

From that time on, I have known that the sense of place is . . . in my blood. I have traveled far and wide, and have made my home elsewhere. But some part of me remains in the hold of northern New Mexico.

As a boy, Momaday saw Indians who kept the old ways and culture. He saw that those people were at peace with themselves and the world around them. They had a strength and beauty that he later found to be missing in the outside world.

After high school, Momaday wasn't sure what to do. He thought about going to West Point. He finally decided to go to the University of New Mexico. There, he began writing poetry. In 1958, he earned a degree in political science.

Momaday received a creative writing fellowship to Stanford University. He earned his Ph.D. in literature from Stanford in 1963. In 1965, Momaday published his first book. It was *The Complete Poems of Frederick Goddard Tuckerman.* The book contains work Momaday did to earn his Ph.D.

Momaday's second book was *The Way to Rainy Mountain.* It tells the story of the Kiowas' journey 300 years ago from the Yellowstone region in Wyoming to the plains area. On the plains, the Kiowas tamed horses and became a highly developed society. The book combines legend, fact, and autobiography.

In the book, Momaday explained the origins of the Kiowa tribe:

> *You know, everything had to begin, and this is how it was. The Kiowas came into the world through a hollow log. They were many more than now, but not all of them got out. There was a woman whose body was swollen up with child, and she got stuck in the log. After that, no one could get through, and that is why the Kiowas are a small tribe in numbers.*

In 1968, Momaday published *House Made of Dawn.* He won the Pulitzer Prize for fiction for this novel. It tells of Abel, an Indian World War II veteran. Abel returns from the war. He is torn between the Indian and white worlds. Only when he returns to his homeland can he heal his soul.

Momaday did not write another novel for 20 years. He wrote poetry and nonfiction. In 1989, he wrote the novel *The Ancient Child.*

Momaday has written many other books. He also has taught in several colleges, including the University of Arizona.

Momaday thinks that Indians have a rich spiritual and cultural heritage. So, Indian writers have much to say to the modern world. Momaday has spent his life preserving his heritage.

His work has a message for all Americans. It is about the relationship of people to the earth. Modern people often don't feel they are a part of nature. But Indians understand people to be as part of nature. Their understanding is based on the idea of harmony in the universe.

Momaday suggests that we need to learn to love nature and to feel we are a part of it. Otherwise, he warns, we shall not live at all.

Momaday holds onto his sense of nature. No matter how many honors he wins, he always returns to his roots to be recharged. His roots are the landscape of Devil's Tower. There, beneath the towering rock column, he feels at one with nature and at peace with himself.

Remembering the Facts

1. Where is Devil's Tower?

2. Why was it important that Momaday was named after Devil's Tower?

3. How did being an only child help Momaday develop skills that he later used in his writing?

4. What effect did the landscape around Jemez, New Mexico, have on Momaday?

5. What did Momaday notice about people who kept the old Indian ways?

6. For which book did Momaday win the Pulitzer Prize for fiction?

7. What message does Momaday's work hold for all people?

Understanding the Story

8. For many years, the white man tried to wipe out Indian ways. Today, Momaday says, it is the Indian way of life that is a good example for white people. In what ways do you think this might be true?

9. One theme of Momaday's work is man's place in nature. Why do you think nature has always been important to Indians?

10. Devil's Tower was chosen as the site for an alien landing in the 1978 movie *Close Encounters of the Third Kind*. Explain why you think this site might have been chosen. Can you think of any other natural sites that might give the same feeling?

Getting the Main Idea

Why do you think Native American literature has value for all Americans?

Applying What You've Learned

Write a legend explaining the existence of a natural feature of the area where you live. (See Momaday's story of the creation of Devil's Tower.)

Ben Nighthorse Campbell
Cheyenne, U.S. Senator

On January 20, 1993, Senator Ben Nighthorse Campbell rode his horse Warbonnet down Pennsylvania Avenue in Washington, D.C. He wore buckskin and a chief's headdress with 72 eagle feathers. Two dozen other Native Americans rode with him. They were from tribes across the United States.

It was inauguration day for President Bill Clinton. Many Cheyennes were happy that Clinton had won the election. But they were also celebrating Campbell's election.

Ben Nighthorse Campbell

Campbell, a Northern Cheyenne, was the first Native American U.S. senator in 60 years.

It was a proud moment for Campbell. He had overcome a childhood of poverty and pain. Through hard work, he had gained success in many areas. Finally, in 1992, he was elected U.S. senator from Colorado. Campbell had become a symbol of hope and pride for all Native Americans.

Campbell was born in Auburn, California, on April 13, 1933. His mother was Mary Vierra. She was a Portuguese immigrant. While still in her teens, she got tuberculosis. She never recovered fully. For the rest of her life, she was in and out of sanitariums—special hospitals for tuberculosis patients.

In 1929, she married a Cheyenne Indian. Her husband was ashamed of being an Indian. He kept it a secret from those outside the family. He was also an alcoholic. He was unable to hold a job for any length of time. Thus, he could not support his family.

Campbell's mother tried to take care of her children. But the family was often without food. One day, the only food left in the house was a can of peas. The mother split the peas between the children. She kept only the juice for herself. Soon, she had no choice. She had to put the children in an orphanage. There, at least, they would be fed.

As time passed, things improved for the family. The father pulled himself together. The children returned home. The family built a store in front of their two-room cabin. Then, they had some amazing good luck. A highway exit was built right beside the store. The store grew. It began making a profit. Finally, the family became more stable.

Campbell's childhood had been hard. But it made him self-reliant and independent. As he said in his autobiography, "If you have nobody to rely on, then you have got to do it yourself." Campbell has been a strong, independent person all his life.

Campbell was a very active teenager. His first job was packing fruit at age 12. Later, he hopped freight trains to go to work with loggers in the Sierra Mountains. He liked work a lot better than going to school. He missed a lot of school. He finally dropped out.

In 1950, Campbell enlisted in the U.S. Air Force. At age 18, he was sent to Korea. The Korean War had started.

While in the Air Force, Campbell worked as a military policeman. He also earned his GED, or general equivalency diploma. But, it bothered him that he had dropped out of high school. Forty years later, he asked the principal of his old high school if he could return for his diploma and march with the class of 1991. The principal agreed as long as Campbell would be the graduation speaker.

In 1953, Campbell came home from Korea. He drove trucks and picked tomatoes. He used to money to go to San Jose State University. He graduated in 1958.

A key to his success in life was judo. He got interested in judo as a teen. He became the youngest fourth-degree black belt in the United States. He won three U.S. judo championships. At the

Pan-American Games, he won a gold medal. He was captain of the U.S. judo team in the 1964 Olympics. But a knee injury cost him the gold medal. Still, he was chosen to carry the American flag in the closing ceremonies.

Judo's discipline helped Campbell succeed in other fields. As a boy, he had learned jewelry making from his father. He perfected his skills. His pieces began to sell for high prices in art galleries.

Today, his Native American jewelry is found in museums and art galleries. It can also be found in the collections of every living U.S. president.

Campbell met his future wife at a judo class. They married and had two children. Campbell supported his growing family with a variety of jobs.

He taught judo. He trained members of the U.S. Olympic judo team. He was a deputy sheriff. He counseled Native American prison inmates. He taught jewelry making. He made and sold jewelry. And he raised and sold championship quarter horses.

Most of these jobs he did at the same time. There was little time for sleep. Finally, his health began to suffer. Doctors told him to take it easy. So, Campbell and his family moved to a ranch in Ignacio, Colorado. There, he raised horses and made jewelry.

Campbell became interested in his Indian roots. He learned he had relatives named Black Horse. They were on the northern Cheyenne reservation in Montana. In 1968, he headed for Lame Deer, Montana. The tribe welcomed him. Campbell felt that he had found his home, at last.

It was by accident that Campbell got into politics. He had gone to the airport near his ranch. He planned to fly to San Francisco to deliver some jewelry. But the plane was grounded by bad weather. While he was waiting, he went to a political meeting to fill some time. A friend of his was going to run for sheriff. Campbell decided to speak on behalf of his friend.

He must have made a good speech. He was asked to run for office himself. The Democrats had not been able to find anyone to run against the very strong Republican candidate for state legislator. Campbell was asked if he'd be willing to run. He agreed. He did not know that no one expected him to win. He was supposed to just fill a spot on the ballot.

Campbell asked a friend if he had a chance of winning. His friend replied, "Oh, I think you have two chances: You have little, and you have none."

That was all Campbell needed to hear. From then on, he knew he would give the race 100 percent. Six months later, he won the election.

Campbell was a popular state legislator. In 1986, he ran for the U.S. House of Representatives and won. Then, in 1992, he was elected to the U.S. Senate.

Campbell has had a colorful career in public office. He has ridden around town on a motorcycle, with his ponytail flying. He has been outspoken in his opinions. Elected as a Democrat, he switched to the Republican party in 1995. But his voting record has not followed any party lines. He has voted the way he thinks is right.

Campbell has looked out for the everyday people in his district. In *Parade* magazine he said:

> *I know the migrant worker who has no money to see a doctor. I know what it is to load trucks. And I know the little guy in the back of the room, slipping behind his classmates. You can talk about hunger, but go hungry for a while. I know it—because it was me.*

Campbell has also fought hard for Indian rights. He led the work to rename the Custer Battlefield in Montana. This name was seen as an insult by Native Americans, who had won the battle. It came to be a symbol of resentment for the many years of mistreatment of Indians.

Thanks mainly to the efforts of Campbell, Congress changed Custer Battlefield to Little Bighorn National Battlefield Monument in 1991. A memorial to the Indians who fought there was planned as well.

Campbell sponsored a bill to start the National Museum of the American Indian in the Smithsonian. The museum's collections represent Indians from the Arctic to the southern tip of South America. The museum is a true celebration of Indian culture.

Campbell has said that all Americans could benefit from living "the Indian way." Indian children are taught not to compete with each other. Instead, they work together for the common good. In his autobiography, Campbell wrote:

> *In the white world, status is a big house, nice car, salary, power . . . but not to Indians. In the Indian world, you are measured by how much you've given to people, how much you help people. You can be in rags and barefoot and still have the most respect within the tribe.*

The story of Ben Nighthorse Campbell is the story of the American dream. It is a rags-to-riches tale of a strong, independent man. Campbell works hard for Indian rights. Indians of all tribes see him as their representative. But Campbell also works hard for all the people in his district.

Remembering the Facts

1. Why did Campbell's mother have trouble taking care of her children?

2. What good thing did Campbell get from his hard childhood?

3. Why did Campbell drop out of high school?

4. What did Campbell have to do in order to march in the high school graduation ceremonies?

5. What did Campbell say was the key to his success in life?

6. Name two jobs Campbell held while his family was young.

7. Why did Native Americans want the Custer Battlefield to be renamed?

8. How did Campbell decide to run for state senator in Colorado?

Understanding the Story

9. Some people do not like the fact that Campbell wears a ponytail and rides a motorcycle. Do you feel his that being different might affect his performance in the Senate?

10. Campbell says that the sport of judo is the key to his success. In what ways do you think success in a sport might lead to success as an adult?

Getting the Main Idea

In what ways is Campbell a good role model for the youth of today?

Applying What You've Learned

Imagine that you are a jewelry maker. Design a piece of jewelry for yourself or a friend. Sketch it. Describe what types of material you will use to make your piece.

Wilma Mankiller
Chief of the Cherokee Nation

For centuries, the Cherokees lived in the southeastern United States. When the whites arrived, the Indians made room for them.

But it was not long before the government began taking Indian land for white settlers. Finally, the government decided to remove the Indians altogether. This decision was known as the *removal policy*.

Some 14,000 Indians were forced to pack up. Under armed guard, they left

Wilma Mankiller

the grasslands and woods of their ancestors. They were herded to the wilds of the Oklahoma Territory. It was a terrible trip. Most of the Indians had to walk all the way in harsh weather, with little food. Nearly 4,000 of them died on the way. Many more died after reaching Oklahoma in a weakened state. The route they walked is known as the Trail of Tears.

Some Cherokees survived the trip. One of these was Wilma Mankiller's great-grandfather. He settled in northern Oklahoma. He raised a family there.

Years later, his great-granddaughter became the first woman chief of the Cherokee nation. Mankiller overcame personal tragedies and violent opposition to win her position. Once in power, she worked hard to make great gains for her people.

Mankiller was born in 1945 in Tahlequah, Oklahoma. This town is the capitol of the Cherokee nation.

Mankiller's father was Cherokee. Her mother was Dutch-Irish. There were 11 children in the family. Mankiller was a middle child. There were many aunts, uncles, and cousins nearby, as well.

The family shared a strong sense of tradition. The children heard stories that had been passed down for generations. The family elders wanted to keep their culture alive for their children.

While rich in culture, the family was very poor. Mankiller's father could not earn enough to keep his family fed.

A new government program sounded like the answer for the family. The idea was to move Indians out of the country into the cities. There, they were promised jobs in which they could earn more money.

In 1957, when Mankiller was 11, the family boarded a train for San Francisco. What a shock was in store for them! They left a home with no telephone, no television, and no indoor plumbing. They also left behind friends, family, and traditions.

They arrived to face life in a San Francisco housing project. It was a strange, hostile place. Mankiller later compared the move to the Trail of Tears:

> *I experienced my own Trail of Tears when I was a young girl. No one pointed a gun at me or at members of my family. But the United States government was again trying to settle the "Indian problem" by removal. I learned through this ordeal about the fear and anguish that occur when you give up your home, your community, and everything you have ever known to move far away to a strange place. I cried for days, not unlike the children who had stumbled down the Trail of Tears so many years before.*

The family stayed in California. Mankiller's father and brother found jobs for $40 a week. The family struggled to get by. The children attended school. Their classmates taunted them and laughed at the family name, Mankiller. The name was once a proud title given to braves who guarded the Indian village from attack.

After high school, Mankiller met Hugo Olaya. Olaya was handsome, fun, and came from a rich family. The two were married and soon had two daughters.

By age 20, Mankiller was settled as a wife and mother. But she was not long content in these roles. She soon knew she had to make some changes.

First, she decided to go back to school. She started college at Skyline Junior College. Later, she went to San Francisco State College. She became more independent. Her marriage failed.

In 1969, a group of Native Americans led by a San Francisco State student seized Alcatraz Island. An old treaty said that unused government lands should go back to Indian use. Since the island was deserted, the protesters took it. They did this to draw attention to the government's mistreatment of native people. They hoped to remind everyone that the land was theirs first.

This event had a big effect on Mankiller. "When Alcatraz occurred, I became aware of what needed to be done to let the rest of the world know that Indians had rights, too," Mankiller said. She knew then that her mission in life would be to serve her people.

Mankiller finished college. She returned to Oklahoma to work for the Cherokee nation. First, she worked as a volunteer. Later, she was hired as a grant writer.

Mankiller was interested in community planning and development. So she formed the Department of Community Development. She knew water and housing were the two biggest needs. So that was where she started.

But Mankiller saw a bigger problem:

> *It was the people's idea that they were in a situation they couldn't do anything about. The single, most important part of my work was trying to get people to maintain a sense of hope and to see that they could come together and actually change their community. They needed to see that they had some control over their own problems.*

One of Mankiller's early projects was the town of Bell, Oklahoma. There, an average person lived on $1,500 a year. Half of the people were without a decent home. One quarter had no indoor plumbing.

Mankiller and her future husband, Charlie Soap, worked with the people of Bell. Together, they built a 16-mile water pipeline that brought water to the town. The project showed the people that they could improve their lives. And it gave Mankiller the experience she later needed in politics.

In 1983, Ross Swimmer ran for chief. He asked Mankiller to be his running mate. Many Cherokees did not think a woman should run for deputy chief. Mankiller's tires were slashed. She got threatening phone calls. Her billboard ads were burned.

Mankiller ignored these threats. She talked about on the issues. The Swimmer/Mankiller team won. Two years later, Swimmer left to take a job in Washington, D.C. Mankiller became chief. In 1987, she was elected chief in her own right. In the 1991 election, she won 83 percent of the vote.

Mankiller did great things for her people. She started a good health care system. The tribe's enrollment tripled. And the tribe developed strong economy. It had an annual budget of $95 million.

In 1995, Mankiller's poor health kept her from running for chief again. But she refused to let a kidney problem, a muscle disease (myasthenia gravis), and an automobile accident stop her altogether.

She was not done working for the Cherokee nation. She has traveled around the country. She has taught others about Cherokee culture, history, and problems. She has worked to correct mistaken ideas many people have about Indians. Wilma Mankiller has kept leading the Cherokee nation into the future.

Remembering the Facts

1. What was the removal policy?

2. What was the Trail of Tears?

3. What was the good side of Mankiller's life in Oklahoma when she was a young girl?

4. Why did the family move to California?

5. What effect did Alcatraz Island have on Mankiller?

6. What did Mankiller see as basic needs in the town of Bell, Oklahoma?

7. Name two things Mankiller accomplished while chief.

   (a)

   (b)

8. What work did Mankiller take up after her term as chief ended?

Understanding the Story

9.   In what ways was Mankiller able to change the attitudes of the Cherokees living in Bell? Why do you think this was important?

10.   Many Cherokees felt that having a woman chief would make their tribe the "laughingstock of the tribal world." Why do you think they felt so strongly? Why did their view change?

Getting the Main Idea

How do you think Mankiller has made a difference in the way young Cherokee women see themselves?

Applying What You've Learned

Friends describe Mankiller as a person who "likes to dance along the edge of the roof." By this they mean that she is willing to take risks to achieve things she believes in. Do you think a good leader must be willing to take risks? Explain your answer in a paragraph.

Fred Begay
Navajo Nuclear Physicist

When Fred Begay was nine, his mother took him to a riverbank near their home. She told him, "We have no food. But you can follow this stream to the Indian school 50 miles away. There you will have free food and clothes and a place to stay."

Fred Begay

The boy said nothing. He turned and began walking. Several days later, he got to the U.S. Bureau of Indian Affairs school. It was two years before he saw his parents again. Many years later, Begay became the first Navajo to earn a doctorate in physics.

Begay was born on the Ute Mountain Indian Reservation. The reservation is in Colorado and Utah. The land is full of beauty. There is Sleeping Ute Mountain, 10,000 feet tall. There are high mesas and canyons. Much of the land is near-desert grasslands. Scrub cedar, oak, and juniper dot the land.

Begay's parents were nomadic. They moved from place to place across the reservation. Begay and his four brothers and sisters slept in the open. The boys were taught to hunt deer and trap rabbits. Getting enough to eat and staying warm in the winter were the main tasks.

Begay's father and mother were Navajo and Ute Indian. They spoke no English. They taught their son to tell time by looking at the sun.

Begay's parents practiced Navajo medicine. They trained their son in their views of religion and medicine. These values are still important to him. Begay said in the *New Mexican,* "If I hadn't become a physicist, I would have probably become a medicine man."

The Indian school was Begay's first real meeting with whites. At the school, he entered a different world. All the students had to wear blue coveralls. They were not allowed to speak Navajo. No Indian religious ceremonies were allowed. Even Begay's name changed. He became Fred Young. And he was given a birth date of July 2, 1932, since his exact birthday was unknown.

At the school, the children were taught a trade. Begay learned farming and blacksmithing. The students were also taught English. But after eight years at the school, Begay still spoke English poorly. He could only read it on a second-grade level.

In 1951, Begay joined the U.S. Army Air Corps. During the Korean War, he served in an air rescue squadron in Korea.

A letter from the Navajo tribal offices in 1955 gave Begay a big chance. It said there were scholarships for Navajos who wanted to attend college. Begay enrolled at the University of New Mexico in 1955. He was 23.

At first, the university did not want to accept him. He had never graduated from high school. The boarding school had been more of a trade school. Finally, the university agreed to give him a try. But he had to attend high school at the same time. Begay went to college during the day and high school at night.

With his weak academic background, Begay struggled in college. During his first semester, his grades were all F's. But within a year, he had pulled up his grades to A's and B's. And he did this while majoring in physics and math.

Begay's early years had given him a scientist's view of the world. In a 1979 interview for *Nova,* he explained why:

> *A scientist looks at the world like a child, always wondering what it is made out of. What are the pieces of the pieces of the pieces?"*

Begay noticed the small details in the world around him.

Begay was a restless student. He was used to moving about. He missed his home. Sometimes, he would leave the university. He would head home to get back in touch with his roots. Always, he returned refreshed.

This system seemed to work for Begay. In 1961, he earned his bachelor's degree. He completed his master's degree in 1963.

The further he went in physics, the more it excited him. As Begay said in *Physics Today,* "I started to have fun." In 1971, he earned his doctorate in nuclear physics. He was the first Navajo to do so.

During the 1960's, Begay worked for NASA, the National Aeronautics and Space Administration. He helped design and build one of the earliest satellites. He also helped design experiments for the early satellites. The experiments were done to study the sun's high-energy rays.

In 1971, Begay joined the physics team at Los Alamos National Laboratory. Los Alamos is the lab where, in 1945, the first atomic bomb was made. The bomb was made by splitting the atom (fission). Begay's work, on the other hand, involved joining atoms to make heat. This was fusion-energy research.

Begay has worked at Los Alamos for more than 25 years. He has focused on harnessing the power of nuclear fusion. Scientists hope that this could be a safer power source than today's nuclear reactors. Begay's work could lead to a way to produce heat that is affordable without harming the environment.

Begay believes that Navajo lore and modern science are alike in many ways. In Navajo legends, the sun is sacred. It is the source of life. It gives guidance and protection.

Begay thinks that the ancient Navajo may have even understood lasers. An ancient sand painting shows warriors with weapons of light rays. Some of these rays are straight, others are zigzag. If Begay could copy the way the sun works, he could bring cheap power to Navajo homes.

In 1979, Begay was the subject of a television show on the series *Nova.* It was called "The Long Walk of Fred Young."

Begay has never forgotten his traditional roots. Every year, he and his wife and seven children have taken their vacation on the Navajo reservation. They have lived in hogans without running water, electricity, or plumbing. In this way, the family has made the old ways a part of their modern life.

Begay advised the Navajo tribe on scientific matters. He has given expert advice on science to the president of the Navajo government. He has been chairman of the Navajo's Environmental Protection Commission. He has been science education adviser to the Navajo Community College. He has chaired the Navajo Science and Engineering Research Council for 23 years.

One of Begay's interests has been helping to improve science and math teaching at the high school level. He has found that fractal geometry makes a good teaching tool. It helps students understand the structure of math. Begay wants teachers to stress creative thinking in math. Students should be allowed to "figure out" answers to problems in their own way.

Begay has spent much of his life improving education for minority students. He serves on a committee to improve math and science programs in all grades at Navajo schools. Since 1991, Begay has helped direct a $10 million math and science project at Arizona State University. This project targets minority college students. It gives them a chance to do research at the university.

Begay has won many awards for his work in science education. In 1992, he won the Ely Parker Award. In 1994, he won the National Science Foundation's Lifetime Achievement Award.

Begay grew up only a few hundred miles from Los Alamos National Laboratory, where he now works. But the two worlds were light years apart. Begay has learned the ways of both worlds. He has become successful and feels at home in both.

Remembering the Facts

1. Where was Fred Begay born?
2. How did the Begay family live?
3. Name two rules at the Indian School.
4. What type of training did the Indian children get at school?

5. Why did Begay have trouble in college at first?

6. What use does Begay hope for from his nuclear research?

7. What kind of work did Begay do for NASA in the 1960's?

8. What is the purpose of the project Begay is involved with at Arizona State University?

Understanding the Story

9. Begay has spent a lot of time helping Navajo college students around the country. Why do you think he has done this?

10. How do you think Begay's upbringing was good training for a future scientist?

Getting the Main Idea

Why do you think Begay is a good role model?

Applying What You've Learned

Imagine that Begay is visiting your school to urge students to pursue careers in science. What message do you think he will bring?

Vocabulary

Mary Musgrove: Creek Interpreter and Diplomat

- Muskogee
- buffer zone
- diplomat
- colony
- treaty
- baptized
- interpreter
- compromise

Tecumseh: Shawnee Warrior and Leader

- mansion
- humane
- persuade
- tract
- kindhearted
- homestead
- disarray
- unity
- torture
- slogan

Sequoyah: Cherokee Linguist

- remarkable
- migrated
- pension
- yacht
- literacy
- silversmith
- obsessed
- crippled
- syllabary
- trademark

Sacagawea: Shoshone Interpreter and Guide

- territory
- anxious
- edible
- emperor
- theory
- monument
- artichoke
- historian
- footnote
- expedition

Sitting Bull: Sioux Chief and Spiritual Leader

- coup
- generations
- homesteaders
- elite
- droughts
- exile
- autograph
- wavered
- identity
- sacred

Chief Joseph: Nez Percé Chief

- salmon
- justice
- surrendered
- barricade
- subdue
- legend
- civilians
- teemed
- unaware
- remote

Sarah Winnemucca: Paiute Indian Rights Activist

- lecturer
- cannibals
- conflicts
- publish
- hastily
- founder
- truce
- treatment
- tuberculosis

Ishi: Yahi Survivor and Research Assistant

- foothills
- chaparral
- collapsed
- canyons
- souvenirs
- matted
- volcano
- anthropology
- sideshows
- adopted
- tuberculosis

Susan LaFlesche Picotte: Omaha Physician

- adapt
- resentful
- missionaries
- alcoholism
- subzero
- physician
- brawls
- anthropologist
- lobby
- activist

Jim Thorpe: Sauk and Fox Athlete

- descendant
- decathlon
- athlete
- endurance
- discipline
- amateur
- carefree
- agility
- eligible
- pentathlon
- Olympic

Maria Martinez: Pueblo Potter

- drought
- archaeologists
- prosperity
- legacy
- population
- potsherd
- revolutionized
- yucca
- techniques
- pueblo
- lifestyle

Annie Dodge Wauneka: Navajo Health Educator

- civilian
- presidential
- civil
- ceremonies
- traditional
- dramatically
- prenatal
- epidemic
- velveteen
- hogan
- honorary
- inspiration
- turquoise
- tuberculosis
- bachelor's degree

N. Scott Momaday: Kiowa Poet and Writer

- estranged
- Pulitzer Prize
- spiritual
- harmony
- creative
- relationship
- prophecy
- autobiography
- heritage
- impact
- novel
- Ph.D.
- advantage

Ben Nighthorse Campbell: Cheyenne, U.S. Senator

- inauguration
- self-reliant
- art galleries
- sponsored
- immigrant
- legislator
- candidate
- sanitarium
- representative
- orphanage
- discipline
- senator

Wilma Mankiller: Chief of the Cherokee Nation

- removal policy
- opposition
- enrollment
- taunted
- ancestor
- hostile
- budget
- tragedy
- anguish
- dedicated

Fred Begay: Navajo Nuclear Physicist

- blacksmithing
- nomadic
- mesa
- academic
- laser
- satellite
- physicist
- nuclear physics
- fission
- fusion
- fractal
- doctorate
- scholarship
- squadron

Answers

MARY MUSGROVE: CREEK INTERPRETER AND DIPLOMAT

Remembering the Facts

1. They built their villages along creeks. So the English named them the Creeks.

2. They had a central location among three nations racing to get land. (The Spanish were pushing north from Florida. The French were moving south from Canada. And the English had much of the Atlantic coast.)

3. The English could build a town at Savannah. They could settle on other lands the Creeks did not need. The English would send traders to the Creek villages. They would be friends.

4. Savannah, Georgia

5. She acted as interpreter for the Creeks and English. She kept the Creeks friendly toward the English.

6. Oglethorpe needed a listening post closer to the Spanish.

7. The Treaty of 1733 was renewed. The Creeks' complaints were settled. They agreed to remain loyal to the English.

8. She got many Creek warriors to join with the English in the fighting.

9. He gave her a diamond ring and 200 pounds. He also hoped to arrange payment for past services and her loss of property while working for him.

10. St. Catherine's Island

Understanding the Story

Answers will vary.

11. The first colonists were tired and sick when they arrive in Georgia. The Creeks could have easily killed them. There could have been fighting, resulting in loss of life by both sides. Also, the Spanish might have taken over Georgia.

12. The Creeks benefited from trading with the English. Their standard of living was improved. They had a ready market

for their goods. They also got new types of goods from the English. The benefits to the English were a peaceful colony and a strong ally.

Getting the Main Idea

Musgrove was a friend and interpreter. She played a big part in every important event in the early years of the colony. Oglethorpe relied on her help. She never let him down.

Applying What You've Learned

She would tell the Creeks that they had been well treated by the English. They had enjoyed years of trading. They had been received as friends. They had been treated with honor. They were likely be worse off if the Spanish took over.

TECUMSEH: SHAWNEE WARRIOR AND LEADER

Remembering the Facts

1. Harrison answered to Tecumseh's speech with lies. The Indian walked out of the talks.

2. Old Piqua, in western Ohio

3. Nearly 1,000 Shawnee left the village after it had been attacked. They moved to Missouri.

4. It gave nearly two thirds of Ohio and part of Indiana to the whites.

5. He wanted to form an Indian alliance that could be strong enough to stand against the whites. He hoped to establish a free independent Indian nation in an area between the United States and Canada.

6. Tecumseh knew he would have to fight the whites.

7. Harrison and his forces defeated the Indians at the Battle of Tippecanoe. Although it was not a major battle, it made Harrison sound good to the public. Harrison used this slogan for his presidential campaign. Tyler was his running mate.

8. The British and their Indian allies were beaten. Tecumseh was killed in the battle.

9. They had lost the war and were not in a position of strength.

10. There was not another strong leader to represent the Indians.

Understanding the Story

Answers will vary.

11. The likelihood of an Indian state would have been much greater. He could have kept the tribes organized and been their spokesperson. United they might have been able to force the creation of an Indian state.

12. Tecumseh was a leader on the battlefield. Also, he was a gifted orator. He was able to inspire others to follow him. He had a clear vision for the future and had a plan to meet it. He had a quick mind and was a good strategist.

Getting the Main Idea

He was one of the strongest Indian leaders of his time. He had a plan for resisting the whites and building a new nation for the Indians. With his death, however, the Indian movement which he began came to a halt.

Applying What You've Learned

Answers will vary.

SEQUOYAH: CHEROKEE LINGUIST

Remembering the Facts

1. silversmithing

2. He saw soldiers reading their mail from home during the War of 1812.

3. He tried to use a different picture for each word. Soon he realized there were too many words for that to work.

4. They thought he was practicing witchcraft. They did not understand. They were fearful of what he was doing.

5. The Eastern Cherokees had burned his home because they thought he was practicing witchcraft. He knew he was no longer welcome there. He decided to make a new start with the Western Cherokees.

6. In an alphabet, each letter can stand for more than one sound. In a syllabary, each symbol stands for one syllable. The sound it makes does not change.

7. He demonstrated how it worked.

8. the Bible and the *Cherokee Phoenix* newspaper

9. He went in search of the lost Cherokees.

Understanding the Story

Answers will vary.

10. Sequoyah's syllabary allowed the Cherokees to become literate. This helped them better adapt to white ways. Writing and reading also brought peace between the Western and Eastern tribes, who could now communicate. It also helped the Cherokees write down tribal lore, which otherwise might have been lost.

11. People often fear things they do not understand. Other members of the tribe did not understand what Sequoyah was doing. They thought he was possessed by an evil spirit.

Getting the Main Idea

Sequoyah was a man of vision. He was true to his vision in spite of what other people thought or said. He kept to his work, believing in himself. Once he was proven right, he was not bitter. His only wish was to share his work with his people so that all could benefit from it.

Applying What You've Learned

Answers will vary.

Students should explain how the demonstration was done. They should tell the members' reaction to it and what action the council decides to take.

SACAGAWEA: SHOSHONE INTERPRETER AND GUIDE

Remembering the Facts

1. *(any two)* to explore the new land; to describe the plants, animals, and people of the new land; to find a water route to the Pacific

2. Her husband, Charbonneau, was hired as an interpreter on condition that she accompany him.

3. The Indians they met would know the group was not a war party when they saw the woman and child. Therefore, they would be less likely to attack the group.

4. She found a variety of vegetables and fruits to give them a balanced diet.

5. horses, supplies, and guides

6. A ship that was supposed to bring them home in comfort did not arrive. They were forced to camp for the winter there and make their way home overland.

7. He adopted him and gave him an education.

8. One theory says that she died in 1812 of a fever at a trading post. Another says that she left her husband and returned to her people, dying at age 100.

Understanding the Story

Answers will vary.

9. The role of women in American history was largely overlooked until the women's rights movement began. Before that, women were only seen in supporting roles. (*Note:* It was during the centennial of the Lewis and Clark expedition that the first research into Sacagawea's life was done. Since then, much more interest has been shown in the role of women in the history of the American West.)

10. The group could have had more illnesses or deaths due to poor nutrition. The group might have been lost in the mountains without the Shoshone guides. The group might have been attacked by hostile Indians. The men could have become depressed and started arguing during the long winter months.

Getting the Main Idea

The expedition opened the American West to further exploration and settlement. Lewis and Clark brought back a wealth of new information about the new land. They also showed there was no easy water route to the Pacific.

Applying What You've Learned

Historians have to be like detectives looking for clues. Written sources include newspaper articles, diaries, and letters. People's memories are another source. Oral traditions, such as stories handed down through generations, can provide clues.

Of course, not all these sources are accurate. Each fact must be verified in several sources. Facts must be viewed in context with the historical times.

SITTING BULL: SIOUX CHIEF AND SPIRITUAL LEADER

Remembering the Facts

1. Very few white men had entered Hunkpapa Sioux territory. Most settlement was occurring to the south along the Oregon trail.

2. He was slow, cautious, and quiet in his manner. He was serious, not physically active.

3. Slow did well in battle by taking coup.

4. They were given a huge part of the Dakota territory to be known as the Great Sioux reservation. Also, they were given permanent hunting rights to an area in Wyoming. No whites were to be allowed on these lands without Indian permission.

5. He said that much of the land that belonged to the Indians was taken away from them in the treaty.

6. He saw enemy soldiers falling upside down into the Sioux camp. This was taken as a sign of a great victory.

7. He was chased across Montana and out of the United States by the U.S. Army.

8. It was feared that a new religion called the ghost dance would cause an Indian uprising. Sitting Bull was known to be the only Indian with enough respect to make such a movement succeed.

9. After Sitting Bull's death, a group of Indians had fled the reservation. The army caught up to them at Wounded Knee. A gun went off, possibly by accident. The army began shooting at the unarmed Indians, killing most of them.

Understanding the Story

Answers will vary.

10. Sitting Bull was a man of vision. He could see that the Indians were losing much more than just land. Their children were becoming part of white culture. Their traditions and way of life were disappearing. Sitting Bull felt that he alone saw what was happening. He felt that he had lost the support of all the others. Thus, he felt that he was the last Indian left.

11. The massacre at Wounded Knee broke the back of the Indian resistance. Now all Indians lived on reservations. They did not have the strength to fight against the overwhelming numbers of white men. They could see that continued resistance was suicide.

Getting the Main Idea

Sitting Bull was more than just a great warrior. He was a man of vision. He was a holy man, the spiritual leader of his people. He could see what was really happening to the Indian people. He remained true to his people, never wavering in his opposition to white influence.

Applying What You've Learned

Arguments for moving to the reservation could include:

There are too many white men; we cannot win against them; we will receive food and shelter on the reservation; we are tired of fighting; we want to raise our families in peace; there are too few warriors left to fight; if we don't cooperate, the government will take our land anyway.

Arguments against moving to the reservation could include:

It's our land; they have no right to take any of it; they have always lied to us; we need to be free to live as we wish; the land they want to give us is not as good as what they are taking away; it is so poor nothing can grow on it or live there; we must continue to fight to preserve our way of life.

CHIEF JOSEPH: NEZ PERCÉ CHIEF

Remembering the Facts

1. They did not wear ornaments in their noses. It was another coastal tribe that did this.

2. It took all but a small part of Nez Percé lands, including the Wallowa Valley.

3. He said never to sell the tribe's land.

4. General Howard was a man of high principle. He tried to convince the government to allow Joseph to stay on his land. Unable to do so, he had to carry out government orders.

5. The Indians had about 150 warriors to fight against 2,000 soldiers. In addition there were 400 women, children, and old people, and huge herds of horses and cattle. Yet they were able to move swiftly and stay ahead of their attackers. They defended themselves using well-planned rear-guard action.

6. There was almost no trail over the mountains. It was a steep, rugged climb. Women, children, old people, and livestock all made the difficult ascent. When their way was blocked, they turned around and went a different route—one which everyone thought was impossible.

7. Defeat was certain. Many of his people had been killed. There was no way out.

8. He tried to get his people returned to their native part of the country. He became a spokesman for his people and gained the admiration and sympathy of many for their cause. Finally, the Nez Percé were able to return to the Northwest because of his efforts.

Understanding the Story

Answers will vary.

9. Joseph and the Nez Percé were never allowed to return to their beloved Wallowa Valley. They had lost their home-land and their way of life. For many years they suffered in the unfamiliar territory of Oklahoma. By the time they were allowed to go back to the Northwest, only 300 of them had survived.

10. In his statement about freedom ("Let me be a free man . . . "), Joseph has given a simple, but complete statement on the freedoms all men desire. He asks for the freedom of

religion. He wants the freedom to speak and think for himself. These basic freedoms are guaranteed all Americans today in the Bill of Rights. Yet, the Indians in those days were denied basic rights. They were confined to their reservations. They were denied their language, their religion, and their culture. Like Martin Luther King, Jr., Chief Joseph asks for the right to be treated as an equal.

Getting the Main Idea

He was admired for his skill in avoiding capture and his courage in battle. Also, the Nez Percé tried to get along peacefully with whites. They fought only to defend themselves. Even the generals who fought against Joseph admired him. They became the most important supporters of the Nez Percé after the war ended.

Applying What You've Learned

Example:

When I entered my homeland, my heart soared. There were the mountains I loved. The forests called out to me. The lake shone below in the sunlight. An eagle soared above me in the sky. As I listened, I could hear the horses neighing in the distance. Closing my eyes, I remembered the days of my youth. My father, my mother, my brothers . . . I could see them all near our tepee with my favorite horse standing nearby in the lush grass.

But now, I must open my eyes. It is my valley, but it is not. I see fences and roads. I see many houses and over there a town. There are no tepees to be seen. I see many, many white people. They are everywhere. No Indians can be seen anywhere.

My valley is there. But for me it no longer exists. I will never be allowed to return there except in my dreams. Everything that my people were is lost forever. We are no more. My heart is so heavy, I feel it must break in two.

SARAH WINNEMUCCA: PAIUTE INDIAN RIGHTS ACTIVIST

Remembering the Facts

1. *(any three)* army scout, interpreter, lecturer, teacher, author, founder of school

2. near Pyramid Lake in northern Nevada

3. He guided Captain John Frémont over the Sierra Nevada Mountains to California. He stayed in California for some time and saw the white man's ways.

4. They did not understand how the whites could communicate by marking on a piece of paper.

5. Many of them were dishonest and greedy. They stole supplies intended for the Indians, who were left poor.

6. She gave lectures and wrote a book.

7. lack of funds

8. She was unable to achieve her goals for her people.

Understanding the Story

Answers will vary.

9. The Peabody School taught the children English and other basic skills. It also taught Indian language and customs. It hoped to help the children to adapt to their new lifestyle, while keeping their own traditions. Native American educators of today would agree with these goals. (In fact, this concept is used as the model in many Indian schools.)

10. Some agents may have hated the Indians as an result of the fighting between Indians and whites. Others may have felt they were savages who had no rights. Many agents did not understand the Indian way of life.

   A dishonest agent could easily get away with mistreating the Indians. The Indians were afraid to fight back because of the overwhelming firepower and numbers of the whites. They knew they would be harshly punished if they tried to fight back.

   Both transportation and communications were unreliable in the American West in the 1800's. There was little communication between Washington, D.C., and the agents. They were free to act as they wished.

Getting the Main Idea

She was tireless in her fight for her people. She was brave. She was a leader at a time when few women were leaders. Her book and lectures awakened the public to the problems of the Indian.

Applying What You've Learned
Answers will vary.
She might include:
- putting on a good show
- dressing in native style to create interest
- demonstrating native dances or crafts
- describing the life of her people before the white man came
- contrasting that with their present life
- describing in detail the poverty of the people
- telling about the cruelty of the agents
- maintaining a calm and sincere tone at all times
- telling how the audience could help

ISHI: YAHI SURVIVOR AND RESEARCH ASSISTANT

Remembering the Facts
1. The country in which they lived is very rugged and full of natural hiding places.

2. The California gold rush of 1848 brought many whites into an area where only the Indians lived before.

3. They kept faithfully to their religion. They made tools and weapons in Stone Age ways. They did not change their way of life, but kept to the old ways.

4. He was like a relic of the Stone Age, completely unlike any other person. He was a novelty, a wild man.

5. He was able to speak some Yana words.

6. in the museum at the university

7. Kroeber wanted him to live as normal a life as possible. Therefore, he avoided publicity or get-rich-quick schemes. Ishi was able to live a normal life by working for his money and then spending it as he wished.

8. At the museum, he gave public demonstrations of Yana life.

9. He showed delight in his friends and everything in his new world. He enjoyed adapting to his new world and learning about it.

10. tuberculosis

Understanding the Story

Answers will vary.

11. He presented a chance to study the life of an ancient people that had never before been studied. He was truly a living relic. He taught the professors his language. He showed them Yana tools and weapons. He enabled them to build a complete, firsthand account of the life of an ancient people.

12. The tragedy is the complete annihilation of a people and their way of life. This might have been prevented if gold fever had not clouded people's thinking.The triumph is that the Yana way of life has been preserved due to Ishi's work with the professors. The Yana homeland has also been preserved for future generations as the Ishi Wilderness in Lassen National Forest.

Getting the Main Idea

The story of Ishi is a unique example of the tragedy that happended to all American Indians as the whites took over their lands. Each Indian tribe has its own story to tell of its struggle with the white man. But the story of Ishi was a more personal account. His people were wiped out. Yet they bravely held to their way of life.

Applying What You've Learned

Answers will vary.

Many thoughts would involve day-to-day survival, for example finding food without being seen. The need to never make a sound, to cover one's tracks could be described. Religion and traditional ways must have given the Yahi strength. The people had to be careful, observant. It had to be a hard life for a child.

SUSAN LaFLESCHE PICOTTE: OMAHA PHYSICIAN

Remembering the Facts

1. He had traveled and been exposed to the white culture.

2. He knew that the only way for the Indian to survive was to adapt to the white world.

3. Women's Medical College in Philadelphia, Pennsylvania

4. She embodied their ideals. She had a strong religious background and a desire to be a doctor. Therefore, she would be a good native missionary.

5. She felt a calling to work among her people. Also, she had agreed to do so in return for a scholarship.

6. (any three) poor roads, primitive means of travel, people were scattered over a large area, mistrust of "white medicine," bad weather, no help, no hospital

7. She built a hospital.

8. She was alarmed at the increasing rate of alcohol abuse. She saw what it did to families.

9. The government held all the land "in trust" for the Indians and managed it for them.

Understanding the Story

Answers will vary.

10. Roles within the tribes were strictly divided on the basis of sex. Men hunted and fought. Women took care of the homes and children. Women did not become chiefs or participate in ceremonies. Women were held to subservient roles while men dominated. Thus, it was rare for a woman to have any type of leadership role.

11. After the Indian wars, Indians were confined to reservations. Their way of life had been taken from them. There was no way for them to support themselves. They became dependent on the government to take care of them. They had little to do. These factors left them wide open for alcohol abuse.

Getting the Main Idea

Susan LaFlesche Picotte worked tirelessly on behalf of her people. She didn't hesitate to speak out for what she thought was right, even if it was not a popular opinion. She spent her entire life working for the health and welfare of her people.

Applying What You've Learned

The pull of alcohol is strong because of the feelings of hopelessness and boredom on the reservation. With little to do, no education, and few positive outlets, it could be easy to slide into the habit of drinking.

Positive influences for a teenager could include: getting an education, developing goals for one's life, developing other hobbies and pastimes, religious training, having friends who do not drink, etc.

Jim Thorpe: Sauk and Fox Athlete

Remembering the Facts

1. Black Hawk

2. They forbade the children to dress in native clothes, speak their native tongues, or practice native customs. Instead, they taught them the white man's customs.

3. *(any three)* football, lacrosse, track, baseball, gymnastics, hockey, wrestling, swimming, handball, basketball, boxing

4. Glenn "Pop" Warner

5. played semipro ball for expense money of $2 a day

6. pentathlon, decathlon

7. baseball, football

8. He was voted the greatest male athlete of the first half of the twentieth century by the Associated Press poll. He was also voted the greatest football player for the same period.

Understanding the Story

Answers will vary.

9. Dark Path: Thorpe's life was full of personal tragedy. He lost his twin brother at age nine. He was orphaned at 16. His first son died at age two. His first two wives divorced him. His Olympic gold medals were taken from him. He was often penniless.

   Bright Path: Thorpe had many victories in his life. He was the greatest athlete of all time, excelling in every sport he tried. He was a person of high ideals and good character. He worked to help children understand the value of sportsmanship. He traveled from school to school at his own expense. He also worked for Native American issues of the day. In the end, Thorpe's medals were restored. He is remembered as a fine athlete and a great person, as well.

10. Thorpe is different because he excelled in so many sports. Today, pro athletes specialize in one sport. Thorpe played both pro baseball and pro football during the same years.

Getting the Main Idea

Thorpe is a good role model because he worked hard to do his best in sports. He kept going through many personal difficulties. He never let his problems get the best of him.

Applying What You've Learned

Many people of the day were outraged by the AAU's actions. They felt that Thorpe was an amateur in track events even though he could be thought of as a pro in baseball. Other athletes of the day had done the same thing he had and not been penalized. Others may have felt that the rules must be followed strictly, no matter what.

MARIA MARTINEZ: PUEBLO POTTER

Remembering the Facts

1. 20 miles northwest of Santa Fe, New Mexico

2. *(any two)* drought, disease, Spanish army, high rate of infant mortality

3. farming

4. Her aunt, Nicolasa Montoya, taught her.

5. Archaeologists were digging at the site of ancient cave dwellings near the village and unearthed the potsherds.

6. They had the opportunity to study examples of ancient pottery. Also, they had time to make and sell their pottery to tourists. This made them realize they could make a living selling their pots.

7. They were a shiny black decorated with engraved flat-black designs.

8. Martinez taught others to make the black pottery. The income and living conditions of the Pueblo Indians were vastly improved.

Understanding the Story

Answers will vary.

9. The village was in effect reborn through the efforts of Martinez. It had been a very poor farming village. Often there was not enough food for everyone. When the Indians began making money with their pottery, their standard of

living improved vastly. People gained some freedom from traditional roles. Men could make pottery. Young people could choose a traditional life or go away to school.

10. Hard times often cause a people to stop practicing an art form. Disease, war, and so on require the people to concentrate on surviving. All of these things happened to the Pueblo Indians. It also became easier to buy plastic bowls. Soon, older people who know the art die without teaching the skills to the next generation.

Getting the Main Idea

Indians had made pottery, jewelry, and rugs for generations. Some of these items were so skillfully made they became an art form. The pottery of Martinez was art. People around the country began to appreciate the beauty of her work and were willing to pay a premium price for it. This, in turn, brought increased attention to the art of other Native Americans.

Applying What You've Learned

Containers could be made of stone, wood, clay, etc. Designs will vary.

ANNIE DODGE WAUNEKA: NAVAJO HEALTH EDUCATOR

Remembering the Facts

1. Presidential Medal of Freedom

2. He made them work hard at traditional jobs around the ranch, such as tending the sheep.

3. because he devoted his life to the betterment of his people

4. She observed an epidemic of flu in the Indian School she attended. Many children died. Wauneka had only a light case. When she recovered, she helped the nurse care for the other children.

5. She knew she could better reach her goals in health care by being in such a position.

6. She went to the public health hospitals. She studied the disease for three months.

7. She wrote a dictionary that translated health words from English to Navajo. If a Navajo word did not exist for an English word, she made up new words.

8. She listened to their ideas. Then she told them that tuberculosis was a white man's and an Indian's disease and that it would take both kinds of medicine to cure it. She got doctors and medicine men to know each other and respect each other's strengths.

9. *(any two)* alcoholism; unhealthful homes with no windows, no plumbing, and dirt floors; better prenatal care; well-baby care

10. alcoholism

Understanding the Story
Answers will vary

11. A mother looks out for the welfare of her children. Wauneka looked out for the welfare of her people. She loved her people and wanted the best for them.

12. Indians were slow to accept white man's medicine. There was a shortage of doctors and hospitals on the reservations. Transportation to health care facilities was a problem for many.

Getting the Main Idea
Wauneka fought for better health care for her people for many years. Her work greatly lessened the incidence of tuberculosis and other diseases on the reservation.

Applying What You've Learned
Answers will vary.
She might have worked on:
- education about the effects of alcoholism on the body
- establishment of treatment centers for alcoholism
- teaching children about alcoholism in schools
- providing free information about alcoholism

N. SCOTT MOMADAY: KIOWA POET AND WRITER

Remembering the Facts

1. in northeast Wyoming

2. because Devil's Tower is a sacred place to the Kiowa

3. He learned to use his imagination to create games and playmates for himself.

4. The land became an important part of his identity.

5. They were at peace with the world around them. They had an inner strength and beauty.

6. *House Made of Dawn*

7. Man is a part of nature. He should live in harmony with the earth.

Understanding the Story

Answers will vary.

8. Indians live in tune with the earth. Whites have often felt that they were masters of the earth. They have used up natural resources. They must learn to live in tune with nature if mankind is to survive.

9. All Indian life was focused on living in harmony with nature. Animals, plants, and the earth were respected as being relations of mankind.

10. Devil's Tower has a mystical presence. The Indians felt and respected it. One cannot see this formation without a feeling of awe and wonder. (For an alternate site, any reasonable answer should be accepted.)

Getting the Main Idea

It is valuable to understand the traditions of each segment of our diverse population. There are universal truths to be found in these writings from which we all can learn.

Applying What You've Learned

Answers will vary.

BEN NIGHTHORSE CAMPBELL: CHEYENNE, U. S. SENATOR

Remembering the Facts

1. She was ill from tuberculosis. Her husband was an alcoholic and couldn't hold a job. The family was very poor.

2. He learned to be self-reliant and independent.

3. He missed too many days of school.

4. He had to agree to be the graduation speaker.

5. judo

6. *(any two)* teaching judo, training members of the U.S. Olympic team, working as a deputy sheriff, counseling Native American prison inmates, teaching jewelry making, selling jewelry, raising quarterhorses

7. They thought the name was an insult to them. Custer had lost the battle. It became a symbol for years of mistreatment by whites.

8. He attended a political meeting to speak on behalf of a friend. Someone was needed to fill a slot on the ballot. He was asked to do it. He accepted.

Understanding the Story

Answers will vary.

9. At first, some people might be surprised at his hairstyle or motorcycle. Some might have a poor first impression. Later, when they got to know him, these things should not matter if he is doing a good job.

10. Success in a sport requires hard work and practice. You must be willing to work hard even when the going gets tough. A person who is hardworking, persistent, and dedicated will find success in many fields.

Getting the Main Idea

Campbell overcame a childhood of poverty and neglect. By hard work and determination, he made a successful career. He is independent. He works hard for what he believes is right. He stands up for his own beliefs.

Applying What You've Learned

Answers will vary.

WILMA MANKILLER: CHIEF OF THE CHEROKEE NATION

Remembering the Facts

1. The removal policy was the U.S. government's practice of moving Indians from any area wanted by whites. Cherokee land in the southeastern United States was given to whites. The Indians were forced to relocate in Oklahoma territory.

2. The Trail of Tears was the journey of the Indians to Oklahoma. Its name reflects the harsh conditions on the trip and the number of resulting deaths.

3. The Mankillers were a large, close family of many generations. They shared a sense of heritage and tradition.

4. The government offered them help in moving. They were to be given jobs and some support.

5. She knew what should be done to let the rest of the world know that Indians have rights, too. She knew her mission in life would be to work for bettering her people.

6. water and housing; also a sense of hope

7. *(any two)* improving water supply, improving housing, developing a health care system, tripling the tribe's enrollment, building the economy of the tribe, increasing the sense of self-worth and self-esteem of tribe members, opening the way to more opportunities for Native Americans

8. teaching others about Cherokee culture, history and problems

Understanding the Story

Answers will vary.

9. The people were living in poverty. They had been mistreated for centuries by the government. Therefore, they had lost their sense of hope. They felt unable to do anything to help themselves. Mankiller gave them a sense of empowerment. This enabled them to do things for themselves.

10. Indian women were never traditionally allowed leadership roles. Mankiller found that when she did things like laying pipe, that was fine. But when she wanted to take a leadership role, that was not fine. When given a chance to prove herself, Mankiller won over most people.

Getting the Main Idea

Mankiller has shown young Cherokee women that there are many roles open to them. She has shown the Cherokees that they can do anything they set their mind to. They do not need to accept their poverty but can work to rise above it.

Applying What You've Learned

A leader must be willing to take risks. To lead, one must take a strong position and be willing to follow it through. This does not mean being reckless, but being willing to listen to and try new ideas.

FRED BEGAY: NAVAJO NUCLEAR PHYSICIST

Remembering the Facts

1. on the Ute Indian Reservation

2. They were nomads, traveling about the reservation. They slept in the open and hunted for food.

3. (any two) wearing blue coveralls, no speaking Navajo, no Indian religious ceremonies

4. They were taught a trade. They learned to read and write some English.

5. He could only read English on a second-grade level. He had not graduated from high school—the Indian school was more of a trade school.

6. He hopes it will be a cheap, environmentally safe source of heat.

7. He helped design and build an early satellite. He designed experiments to study the sun's high energy rays.

8. It targets minority college students who study science and math.

Understanding the Story

Answers will vary.

9. Fred Begay hopes to help Indian students succeed in math and science. Begay knows that many of these students will drop out without extra help.

10. As a child, Begay learned to pay close attention to details. He became a keen observer. He developed a love of nature. He became curious to learn how things in nature work. His parents taught him the ways of the medicine man. This required him to learn a great deal of material in great detail. All of these things contributed to his having the right approach to learning science.

Getting the Main Idea

Begay took advantage of the opportunities that came his way. Instead of finding reasons he could not succeed, he kept trying. He did not let his initial failure stop him. He began his college education in 1955 and received his Ph.D. in 1971. He didn't give up in his quest for an education.

Begay has remained true to his roots and true to his people. He still practices many of his native ways. And he devotes time to helping other Navajos succeed in science.

Applying What You've Learned

Answers will vary.

Additional Activities

Mary Musgrove: Creek Interpreter and Diplomat

1. Find out more about the lifestyle of the ancient Creek Indians. They built great Indian mounds, some even larger than the great pyramids of Egypt. In all, almost 100,000 mounds can be found in the central, southeastern, and western United States.

2. Read about the lifestyle of the Indians in the Creek Confederacy which existed when the first white settlers arrived in the New World.

3. Read more about one of these famous Creek Indians:

   Chief Tuscalusa (sixteenth century)
   Chief Tomochichi (early seventeenth century)
   Alexander McGillivray (late eighteenth century)

4. In the 1830's, the Creeks were forced to move to Oklahoma by the Indian Removal Act. Today there are about 15,000 Creeks living in the east central part of Oklahoma. For information, write:

   Creek Nation of Oklahoma
   P.O. Box 580
   Okmulgee, OK 74447

5. Read more about the role the Indians played in the American Revolution (1775–1783).

6. The Creeks rebelled against the settlers' moving into their ands by starting the Creek War of 1813. The war ended as Andrew Jackson defeated the Creeks at the Battle of Horseshoe Bend. The Creeks lost about two thirds of their remaining territory after this battle. Find out more about it.

7. The Seminoles were a southern branch of the Creeks, located in Florida. They were all but wiped out during the Seminole Wars of 1816 and 1835. Read more about the story of Chief Osceola and the Seminole Wars.

Tecumseh: Shawnee Warrior and Leader

1. Read more about William Henry Harrison, ninth president of the United States (1773–1841). He died only one month after being inaugurated.

2. Find out more about Tecumseh's famous brother Lalawethika, also known as Tenskwatawa, the Open Door. He began a religious revival which became known as the Indian movement and attracted large number of followers. He was also known as the Shawnee Prophet.

3. Read about the War of 1812 and the role of the Indians in it.

4. Many places and things have been named in honor of Tecumseh. Cities in Oklahoma, Kansas, Michigan, and Ontario bear his name. There is also a Tecumseh Natural Area in Ohio. Find these places on a map.

5. Read one of the many fine biographies on the life of Tecumseh.

Sequoyah: Cherokee Linguist

1. Look up more information about the syllabary Sequoyah developed. Try putting together some words using it.

2. Find out more about the Trail of Tears, when the Cherokees were forcibly removed from their homes in the 1830's and sent to Oklahoma to a reservation.

3. Read about the War of 1812 and the role of the Cherokees as allies to white Americans in this war.

4. Find out about the writing system used by the ancient Mayans in Mexico.

5. Read about the giant redwood trees named in Sequoyah's honor, the California sequoias.

6. The facts presented in this story are generally agreed upon by historians. There are, however, other views of Sequoyah's life. For another point of view, you may wish to look at one or more of these books.

   (a) George E. Foster, in his 1885 book *Se-Quo-Yah: The American Cadmus and Modern Moses,* makes Sequoyah into a romantic dashing hero.

   (b) Traveler Bird's 1971 book *Tell Them They Lie: The Sequoyah Myth* claims that a lost tribe of Cherokees came out of the West and presented the Cherokees with a language on thin gold plates. (No proof exists to support this idea.)

(c)   A number of other books have been written on the life of Sequoyah, which follow his life as given in this story.

Sacagawea: Shoshone Interpreter and Guide

1.   Read more about the Lewis and Clark expedition. On a map, trace the route of their 8,000-mile journey.

2.   Read the story of how the Louisiana Purchase was made.

3.   Sacagawea State Park in Washington State is the site where the party camped before beginning their voyage down the Columbia River. Its visitor center has details of the expedition.

4.   Read more about the life of Sacagawea's son, Jean Baptiste Charbonneau, best known as Pomp.

5.   The Lewis and Clark Interpretive Center at Fort Canby, Washington, has been called the best exhibit about the expedition. Nearby, Fort Clatsop has been rebuilt. For information, write:

     Fort Clatsop National Memorial
     Route 3, Box 604-WC
     Astoria, OR 97103

6.   Another Indian woman, Marie Dorion, guided explorers on an expedition to Astoria, Oregon (1811–1812). Find out more about Marie Dorion's story.

7.   The Lewis and Clark Historic Trail follows the entire route of the expedition. You can follow the trail by boat, by foot, by horseback, or by car. Motor vehicle routes are marked with rectangular signs bearing the silhouette of Lewis and Clark. The trail connects a series of memorials, museums, visitor centers, exhibits, and historic sites. The National Park Service publishes free information about the Lewis and Clark Historic Trail. Write them at:

     Lewis and Clark National Historic Trail
     700 Rayovac Drive, Suite 100
     Madison, WI 53711.

Sitting Bull: Sioux Chief and Spiritual Leader

1. Read an account of the Battle of the Little Bighorn. Write a brief report on it.

2. Find out more about other famous Sioux leaders including Red Cloud, Crazy Horse, Spotted Tail, Gall, Bull Owl, and Rain-in-the-Face.

3. In the Black Hills, a few miles from Mount Rushmore (where the heads of presidents are carved), is a huge sculpture of Crazy Horse. The carving in Thunderhead Mountain is 563 feet high and 641 feet long. Find out more about this monument.

4. Find the following on a map: the Black Hills (South Dakota), the Bighorn Mountains (Montana), the Little Bighorn River (southeastern Montana), the Platte River, and the Powder River.

5. Find the following Sioux reservations on maps. Note that several of these date from 1868, the Fort Laramie treaty we read about in the story.

   South Dakota: Cheyenne River Reservation (1889), Crow Creek Reservation (1863), Flandreau Reservation (1935), Lower Brule Reservation (1868), Pine Ridge Reservation (1868), Rosebud Reservation (1868), Sisseton Reservation (1867), Yankton Reservation (1853)

   North Dakota: Devil's Lake Reservation (1867), Standing Rock Reservation (1868)

   Montana: Fort Peck Reservation (1873)

   Minnesota: Lower Sioux Reservation (1887), Prairie Island Reservation (1887), Shakopee Community (1969), Upper Sioux Community (1938)

6. Read about some of the U.S. Army Indian fighters such as General Nelson Miles, General Terry, General George Armstrong Custer, General Henry H. Sibley, General Alfred Sully, General George Crook, or Major Reno.

7. Find out more about Buffalo Bill Cody and his Wild West Show.

8. Read more about the Battle at Wounded Knee.

9. Several books have been written about the life of Sitting Bull (see "References" for a partial list). Read one of them and report to the class facts you discover which were not included in the story in *16 Extraordinary Native Americans.*

10. Read more about Red Cloud's war against the opening of the Bozeman Trail.

11. Find out more about the ghost dance of the late 1880's. A Paiute prophet called Wovoka told the Indians that by joining his new religion and dancing the ghost dance, they would find eternal peace.

Chief Joseph: Nez Percé Chief

1. In 1968, Congress created the National Trails System. The Nez Percé Trail, Nee-Me-Poo, runs 1170 miles from the vicinity of Wallowa Lake, Oregon, to the Bear Paw Battlefield near Chinook, Montana. It was named a National Historic Trail in 1986. Find out more about this trail. If you were planning a hike, which parts would you most like to cover?

2. The Nez Percé National Historical Park and Museum preserves the history of the Nez Percé people. It was established in 1965. For more information, write:

   Nez Percé National Historical Park and Museum
   P.O. Box 93
   Spaulding, ID, 83551
   (208) 843-2261

3. Locate the Chief Joseph Highway on a map of Montana.

4. Locate the following Nez Percé reservations on a map:

   Washington state: Colville Reservation in Nespelem

   Idaho: Nez Percé Reservation in Lapwai

5. Read more about General O.O. Howard, General Nelson Miles, Colonel John Gibbon, or Colonel Sturgis.

6. Find out more about the early history of Yellowstone Park, including its establishment as our first national park in 1872.

7. Read more about other Nez Percé chiefs including White Bird, Looking Glass, and Too-hool-hool-zote.

Sarah Winnemucca: Paiute Indian Rights Activist

1. The town of Winnemucca, Nevada, is named in honor of the Winnemucca family. Find this town on a map. Find out more information about the town.

2. Find the following Paiute reservations on a map of Nevada: Pyramid Lake Reservation (1874), Duck Valley Reservation (1877), Fallon Colony and Reservation (1887), Fort McDermit Reservation (1892), Los Vegas Colony (1911), Lovelock Colony (1907), Moapa Reservation (1875), Summit Lake Reservation (1913), Walker River Reservation (1871), Winnemucca Colony (1917), Yerington Colony and Reservation (1836)

3. Sarah Winnemucca's book *Life Among the Paiutes: Their Wrongs and Claims* was reprinted in 1969 by the Chalfant Press. Look for a copy of this book at your local library. Read Winnemucca's story in her own words.

4. In his book *Famous Indian Chiefs I Have Known,* General O.O. Howard (read more about him in the story on Chief Joseph) wrote about his friendship with Winnemucca. Get a copy of this book and read what he says about her.

5. Read more about Captain Truckee. The town of Truckee, Nevada, is named in his honor. Find it on a map.

6. Find out more about the explorer John C. Frémont, friend of Captain Truckee.

7. One Indian agent who was a good man and treated the Indians well was Sam B. Parrish. Find out more about how Parrish worked with the Paiutes.

8. Find the following places that were important in Winnemucca's life on a map: Pyramid Lake, Nevada; the Sierra Nevada Mountains; Sacramento, California; Lovelock, Nevada (site of Winnemucca's school).

9. One favorite food of the Paiutes was the pine nut. Find out where these come from and how they are used as food.

Ishi: Yahi Survivor and Research Assistant

1. Read an account of Ishi's life. Theodora Kroeber's book *Ishi in Two Worlds: A Biography of the Last Wild Indian in North America* is the best biography of Ishi. Three years later

Kroeber wrote *Ishi: Last of His Tribe.* Both of these make great reading.

2. The Ishi Wilderness is a 41,000 acre tract in the Lassen National Forest in Northern California. It was set aside in 1984 to preserve the homeland of the Yana Indians. Information is available from:

> Lassen National Forest Supervisor's Office
> 55 South Sacramento Street
> Susanville, CA 96130
> (916) 257-2151
>
> or
>
> Almanor Ranger District Lassen National Forest
> P.O. Box 767
> Chester, CA 96020

3. Read more about the 1848 California Gold Rush.

4. An Ishi exhibit is at the Phoebe Apperson Hearst Museum of Anthropology at the University of California, Berkeley. For information write:

> Phoebe Hearst Museum of Anthropology
> 103 Kroeber Hall
> University of California
> Berkeley, CA 94720-3712
> (510) 642-3681

Susan LaFlesche Picotte: Omaha Physician

1. Read about other Native American woman doctors. Some examples are: Rosa Minoka Hill (Mohawk) and Lucille Johnson Marsh (Tuscarora).

2. Find out more about one of these Native American physicians: Charles Alexander Eastman (Santee Sioux), Carlos Montezuma (Yavapai), or Everett Ronald Rhoades (Kiowa).

3. Read about one of the other members of Picotte's family: Iron Eye, or Joseph LaFlesche (chief), Susette LaFlesche (activist and writer), Rosalie LaFlesche (businesswoman), Marguerite LaFlesche (teacher), or Francis LaFlesche (anthropologist).

4. Find the Omaha reservation on a map of Nebraska. Locate the town of Walthill.

5. For information about the Omaha tribe, write:

    The Omaha Tribe Council
    P.O. Box 368
    Macy, NE 68039

6. Find out more about the Hampton Normal and Agricultural Institute. It had been founded to educate black freedmen. But in Picotte's day, it was teaching Indians, as well.

7. Find out more about the problem of alcoholism on reservations and what is being done about it.

Jim Thorpe: Sauk and Fox Athlete

1. Glenn "Pop" Warner was great coach who did much to make football what it is today. Read more about him. Write a paragraph telling some of Warner's contributions to the game of football.

2. Find out more about the Haskell Institute in Kansas or the Carlisle Indian Industrial School in Pennsylvania, which closed in 1918.

3. Find out more about Jim Thorpe's football team by reading: *Jim Thorpe and the Oorang Indians: The NFL's Most Colorful Franchise.* (The book is by Robert Whitman, Hubbard Publishers, 1984.)

4. Write a paragraph telling whether you think the Amateur Athletic Union was right to make an example of Jim Thorpe by taking away his medals. Explain your reasons.

5. Find out more about the life of Charles Curtis, vice president of the United States under Herbert Hoover. Curtis was a Native American and a member of the Kansa/Kaw-Osage tribe.

6. Find out more about the town of Jim Thorpe, Pennsylvania. Write a tour guide describing the town and its many tourist attractions.

7. Discuss whether Olympic participaton should be limited to amateur athletes.

8. Find out more about Black Hawk, Thorpe's famous ancestor. Write a paragraph telling how the two were alike.

9. If Thorpe were an athlete today, he would probably be very rich. Instead, he lived in poverty for much of his life. Write a paragraph telling why you think he never was able to gain wealth with all his fame.

10. View the movie *Jim Thorpe—All-American* (1950).

11. Indian boarding schools of Thorpe's day tried to make Indian children "white." Explain why they were so eager to take the Indians' culture away.

Maria Martinez: Pueblo Potter

1. Read about the ancient Cliff Dwellers called the Anasazi. These people built entire cities into the cliffs centuries ago. Suddenly, in the thirteenth century, they left their cliff homes. No one knows why. But their beautiful buildings in the cliffs remain today, vacant. The ruins at Mesa Verde are one outstanding example of cliff dwellings.

2. Find pictures of the pottery of Martinez. The book *The Living Tradition of Maria Martinez,* by Susan Peterson, is a good source.

3. Read about Popovi Da, Martinez's son, also a famous artist.

4. For more information about San Ildefonso and its museum, write:

   Pueblo of San Ildefonso
   Route 5, Box 315-A
   Santa Fe, NM 87501
   (505) 455-2273

5. Choose a Native American art form and read more about it. Report on it to the class. Some examples are: beadwork, pottery making, quillwork, rug making, painting, basket making, textile weaving, jewelry, ribbonwork, etc.

Annie Dodge Wauneka: Navajo Health Educator

1. Read about the Navajo tribe. It is the largest Native American tribe. The main Navajo reservation spreads over nearly 14,000,000 acres in northeastern Arizona.

2. Find the Navajo reservations on a map:

   In Arizona: Navajo Reservation (1868) (the largest reservation)

   In New Mexico: Alamo Reservation (1868), Canoncito Reservation (1868), Ramah Reservation (1868)

3. Find out more about Navajo rugs and how they are woven.

4. Find out about Navajo jewelry. Made from silver and decorated with turquoise, this fine jewelry is prized the world over.

5. Read more about the disease of tuberculosis.

6. Find out more about the Medal of Freedom, its establishment, and some of the people who have won it.

7. Navajo is a hard language to learn. Most young Navajo children today have not learned to speak their traditional tongue. During World War II, Navajo marines were able to send radio messages in Navajo. The Japanese were never able to break this code. Find out more about the Navajo code-talkers and their special contribution to the war effort.

N. Scott Momaday: Kiowa Poet and Writer

1. Read one of Momaday's books of fiction or poetry. These include:

    House Made of Dawn, New York: Harper & Row, 1968.

    The Way to Rainy Mountain, Albuquerque: University of New Mexico Press, 1969.

    Colorado: Summer, Fall, Winter, Spring. Chicago: Rand McNally, 1973.

    Angle of Geese and Other Poems, Boston: David R. Godine, 1974.

    The Names: A Memoir. New York: Harper & Row, 1976.

    The Ancient Child. New York: Doubleday, 1989.

    In the Presence of the Sun: A Gathering of Shields. New York: St. Martin's Press, 1992.

2. Write a "tour guide" describing the sights around the Devil's Tower National Monument. Write to:

    Department of Tourism
    Wyoming Department of Commerce
    I-25 at College Drive
    Cheyenne, WY 82002

3. Find out more about the Kiowa people and their history. Write a brief report on your findings.

4. Read one of Momaday's poems. Write a paragraph discussing the poem. Share the poem and your analysis with the class.

5. Native Americans passed on their history from one generation to the next by storytelling. Tell a story from your family tradition to the class.

6. Kiowas and some other tribes had another way to preserve their history. They kept winter counts—picture records that showed the single most important event that happened to the tribe during a one-year period. The event to be recorded was decided by the elders of the tribe. For example, for a year in which the snow was unusually deep, the picture might be about a big snowstorm. The pictures for many years were drawn on a single piece of leather. The winter count gave the Indians a way of keeping track of time, as well as preserving history.

    A story went with the pictured event. This was not written down but was memorized by the tribe historian who presented it orally. The historian might know the history for many years. The historian learned the story of each event from the father and grandfather. New events were added each year.

    The Kiowa elder who named N. Scott Momaday Tsoai-talee after Devil's Tower had the Kiowa winter count, which went back to 1833. Momaday learned much about the history of his people from that book. Draw a winter count for your own life. Make one pictograph or drawing for each year of your life. (All of these should fit on one side of a piece of paper.)

Ben Nighthorse Campbell: Cheyenne, U.S. Senator

1. Find out more about tuberculosis, the disease that Campbell's mother suffered from most of her life. How was it treated in the sanitariums?

2. When Campbell was a child, there was much prejudice in California against people of color, including Indians. Many people hid their Indian heritage. Today, people are usually proud of their Indian background. Write a paragraph telling why you think this has changed.

3. Campbell credited the sport of judo with being the key to his success. Judo "gave his life purpose, channeled his aggressions, and taught him self-discipline." Find out more about this sport and report on it to the class.

4. When Campbell's wife found out he would be entering politics, she said, "Now are you going to have to learn to lie?" Explain what you think she meant. Do you think most politicians are honest or not? Explain your answer.

5. Read about the Battle of the Little Bighorn.

6. Find out about the National Museum of the American Indian in the Smithsonian Museum in Washington, D.C.

7. Regarding Indian roles today, Campbell said, "The buffalo are not coming back." Write a paragraph explaining what he meant.

8. The year 1992 marked the five-hundredth anniversary of Columbus discovering America. Many Native Americans were not happy with the idea of celebrations honoring Columbus. Discuss why they would feel this way.

Wilma Mankiller: Chief of the Cherokee Nation

1. Native Americans today look and act much like other Americans, although they have their own culture. But many people have wrong ideas about Indians. Make a list of these stereotypes.

2. Find out about the Treaty of New Echota, which gave all Cherokee lands to the white man in 1836.

3. Read more about the Trail of Tears.

4. Many movies about cowboys and Indians were made in the 1950's and 1960's. These movies show Indians as savages. Write a paragraph telling how you think such movies added to negative ideas about Indians.

5. Read about the American Indian Movement (AIM).

6. Read more about the occupation of Alcatraz. Write a paragraph telling of your findings.

7. Wilma Mankiller has become a symbol of success for Cherokee women and other women everywhere. Why are her accomplishments so notable?

8. Many Native Americans live in two worlds: the non-Indian world and their Indian heritage. Write a paragraph telling why this could be confusing for young Native Americans.

9. In 1979, Mankiller was badly injured in a car accident. Recovery took many months. During the long healing process she adopted what is called "a Cherokee approach to life." That means "being of good mind." When one is of "good mind" one accepts what has happened and turns it into a better path. Write a paragraph telling how attitude might affect recovery from an injury or illness.

10. Mankiller stated in her autobiography that she thinks of herself as "the woman who lived before and the woman who lives after" the accident. Write a paragraph telling how a narrow brush with death might change a person.

Fred Begay: Navajo Nuclear Physicist

1. Read about other well-known Native American scientists. Examples are Clifton Poodry, Jerrel Yakal, Wilfred F. Denetclaw, Frank C. Dukepoo.

2. Find out about how thermonuclear fusion is being studied as a cheap and environmentally sound source of heat and electricity.

3. The Ute Mountain Tribal Park includes cliff dwellings and pueblos. For more information, write:

    Tribal Park
    Towaoc, CO 81223
    (800) 847-5485

4. For more information about the Four Corners Area, contact the one of the following tourism boards:

    Navajo Tourism Dept.
    P.O. Box 663
    Window Rock, AZ 86515
    (602) 871-6659

    Southwest Colorado Travel
    P.O. Box 2102
    Montrose, CO 81402
    (800) 933-4340

    Farmington Visitors Bureau
    203 W. Main, Suite 401
    Farmington, NM 87305
    (800) 448-1240

    Moab Information Center
    Center and Main St.
    Moab, UT 84532
    (800) 635-MOAB

5. Find out what fractal geometry is.

6. Find out more about how Navajo sand paintings are made.

7. Read about the work done at Los Alamos National Laboratory in New Mexico.

8. Read the story of the development of the first atomic bomb at Los Alamos National Laboratory.

9. For more information about Native Americans in Science and Engineering, contact:

> American Indian Science and Engineering Society
> 1630 30th Street Suite 301
> Boulder, CO 80301

> Society for the Advancement of Chicanos and Native Americans in Science
> University of California
> 1156 High Street
> Santa Cruz, CA 95064

References

Mary Musgrove: Creek Interpreter and Diplomat

Coleman, Kenneth. *Colonial Georgia: A History.* New York: Charles Scribner's Sons, 1976.

Corkran, David H. *The Creek Frontier: 1540–1783.* Norman, OK: University of Oklahoma Press, 1967.

Coulter, E. Merton. *Georgia: A Short History.* Chapel Hill, NC: The University of North Carolina Press, 1933.

Gridley, Marion E. *American Indian Women.* New York: Hawthorn Books, Inc., 1974, pp. 33–38.

Jackson, Harvey H. and Phinizy Spalding. *Forty Years of Diversity: Essays on Colonial Georgia.* Athens, GA: The University of Georgia Press, 1984.

Tecumseh: Shawnee Warrior and Leader

Dockstader, Frederick. *Great North American Indians: Profiles in Life and Leadership.* New York: Van Nostrand Reinhold Co., 1977, pp. 290–292.

Drake, Benjamin. *Life of Tecumseh.* 1858; reprinted, North Stratford, NH: Ayer Company, 1988.

Eckert, Allan W. *A Sorrow in Our Heart.* New York: Bantam, 1992.

Notable Native Americans. Detroit: Gale Research, 1995, pp. 426-430.

Roland, Albert. *Great Indian Chiefs.* New York: Crowell-Collier Press, 1966, pp. 93–112.

Sugden, John. *Tecumseh's Last Stand.* Norman, OK: University of Oklahoma Press, 1985.

Sequoyah: Cherokee Linguist

Coblentz, Catherine Cate. *Sequoya.* New York: Longmans, Green & Co., 1946.

Dockstader, Frederick J. *Great North American Indians: Profiles in Life and Leadership.* New York: Van Nostrand Reinhold Co., 1977, pp. 259–261.

Heuman, William. *Famous American Indians.* New York: Dodd, Mead & Co., 1972, pp. 44–50.

Hirschfelder, Arlene, and Martha Kreipe de Montano. *The Native American Almanac.* New York: Prentice Hall General Reference, 1993, pp. 83–84.

Notable Native Americans. Detroit: Gale Research, 1995, pp. 391–394.

Wheeler, Jill C. *The Story of Sequoyah.* Bloomington, MN: Abdo & Daughters, 1989.

Sacagawea: Shoshone Interpreter and Guide

Burt, Olive. *Sacajawea.* New York: Franklin Watts, 1978.

Dockstader, Frederick J. *Great North American Indians: Profiles in Life and Leadership.* New York: Van Nostrand Reinhold Co., 1977, pp. 248–249.

Gridley, Marion E. *American Indian Women.* New York: Hawthorn Books, Inc., 1974, pp. 47–53.

Notable Native Americans. Detroit: Gale Research, 1995, pp. 374–377.

Snyder, Gerald S. *In the Footsteps of Lewis and Clark.* Washington: The National Geographic Society, 1970.

Sitting Bull: Sioux Chief and Spiritual Leader

Black, Sheila. *Sitting Bull and the Battle of the Little Bighorn.* NJ: Silver Burdett Press, 1989.

Dockstader, Frederick J. *Great North American Indians.* New York: Van Nostrand Reinhold, 1977, pp. 266–269.

Freedman, Russell. *Indian Chiefs.* New York: Holiday House, 1987, pp. 115–142.

Heuman, William. *Famous American Indians.* New York: Dodd, Mead and Co., 1972, pp. 109–117.

Notable Native Americans. Detroit: Gale Research, 1995, pp. 399–402.

Taylor, William O. *With Custer on the Little Bighorn.* New York: Viking Penguin, 1996.

Utley, Robert M. *The Lance and the Shield: The Life and Times of Sitting Bull.* New York: Henry Holt, 1993.

Chief Joseph: Nez Percé Chief

Davis, Russell, and Brent Ashabranner. *Chief Joseph: War Chief of the Nez Percé.* New York: McGraw-Hill Book Co., 1962.

Dockstader, Frederick J. *Great North American Indians: Profiles in Life and Leadership.* New York: Van Nostrand Reinhold Co., 1977, pp. 128–130.

Freedman, Russell. *Indian Chiefs.* New York: Holiday House, 1987, pp. 91–114.

Heuman, William. *Famous American Indians.* New York: Dodd, Mead and Co., 1972, pp. 78-93.

Chief Joseph, Nez Percé. *Chief Joseph's Own Story.* April 1879. *North American Review.*

Notable Native Americans. Detroit: Gale Research, 1995, pp. 281–219.

Sarah Winnemucca: Paiute Indian Rights Activist

Dockstader, Frederick J. *Great North American Indians: Profiles in Life and Leadership.* New York: Van Nostrand Reinhold Co., 1977, pp. 337–339.

Gridley, Marion E. *American Indian Women.* New York: Hawthorn Books, Inc., 1974, pp. 54–61.

Howard, O.O. *Famous Indian Chiefs I Have Known.* Century Co., 1908.

Morrison, Dorothy. *Chief Sarah: Sarah Winnemucca's Fight for Indian Rights.* New York: Atheneum, 1980.

Morrow, Mary Frances. *Sarah Winnemucca.* Milwaukee: Raintree Publishers, 1990.

Notable Native Americans. Detroit: Gale Research, 1995, pp. 460–462.

Winnemucca, Sarah. *Life Among the Piutes: Their Wrongs and Claims.* 1883; reprinted, New York: Chalfant Press, 1969.

Ishi: Yahi Survivor and Research Assistant

Dockstader, Frederick J. *Great North American Indians: Profiles in Life and Leadership.* New York: Van Nostrand Reinhold Co., 1977.

Heizer, Robert F., and Theodora Kroeber, ed., *Ishi the Last Yahi: A Documentary History.* Berkeley, CA: University of California Press, 1979.

Kroeber, Theodora. *Ishi in Two Worlds: A Biography of the Last Wild Indian in North American.* Berkeley, CA: University of California Press, 1961.

———. *Ishi: Last of His Tribe.* Berkeley, CA: Parnassus Press, 1964.

Meyer, Kathleen Allan. *Ishi: The Story of an American Indian.* Minneapolis: Dillon Press, Inc., 1981

Notable Native Americans. Detroit: Gale Research, 1995, pp. 206–209.

Susan LaFlesche Picotte: Omaha Physician

Dockstader, Frederick J. *Great North American Indians: Profiles in Life and Leadership.* New York: Van Nostrand Reinhold Co., 1977, pp. 143–145.

Gridley, Marion E. *American Indian Women.* New York: Hawthorn Books, Inc., 1974, pp. 74–81.

Notable Native Americans. Detroit: Gale Research, 1995, pp. 238–241.

Jim Thorpe: Sauk and Fox Athlete

Berontas, Bob. *Jim Thorpe: Sauk and Fox Athlete.* New York: Chelsea House Publishers, 1992.

Dockstader, Frederick J. *Great North American Indians: Profiles in Life and Leadership.*

New York: Van Nostrand Reinhold, 1977.

Hahn, James, and Lynn Hahn. *Thorpe! The Sports Career of James Thorpe.* Mankato, MN: Crestwood House, 1981.

Richards, Gregory B. *Jim Thorpe, World's Greatest Athlete.* Chicago: Children's Press, 1984.

Rivinus, Edward F. *Jim Thorpe.* Milwaukee: Raintree Publishers, 1990.

Maria Martinez: Pueblo Potter

Gridley, Marion E. *American Indian Women.* New York: Hawthorn Books, Inc., 1974, pp. 105–114.

Gridley, Marion E. *Contemporary American Indian Leaders.* New York: Dodd, Mead & Co., 1972, pp. 123–128.

Marriott, Alice. *Maria, the Potter of San Ildefonso.* Norman: University of Oklahoma Press, 1945.

Nelson, Mary Carroll. *Maria Martinez.* Minneapolis: Dillon Press, 1972.

Notable Native Americans. Detroit: Gale Research, 1995, pp. 263–264.

Peterson, Susan. *The Living Tradition of Maria Martinez.* Tokyo: Kodansha International, 1977.

Annie Dodge Wauneka: Navajo Health Educator

Gridley, Marion E. *American Indian Women.* New York: Hawthorn Books, Inc., 1974, pp. 119–130.

Gridley, Marion E. *Contemporary American Indian Leaders.* New York: Dodd, Mead & Co., 1972, pp. 186–194.

Nelson, Mary Carroll. *Annie Wauneka.* Minneapolis: Dillon Press, Inc., 1972.

Notable Native Americans. Detroit: Gale Research, 1995, pp. 453–454.

N. Scott Momaday: Kiowa Poet and Writer

Contemporary Authors, New Revision Series. vol. 34, pp. 313–316.

Current Biography. New York: H.W. Wilson Company, 1975, pp. 281–283.

Momaday, N. Scott. *House Made of Dawn.* New York: Harper & Row, 1968.

Momaday, N. Scott. *The Way to Rainy Mountain.* Albuquerque: University of New Mexico Press, 1969.

Notable Native Americans. Detroit: Gale Research, 1995, pp. 273–275.

Something About the Author, vol. 48, Detroit: Gale Research, 1987, pp. 158–162.

Ben Nighthorse Campbell: Cheyenne, U.S. Senator

Notable Native Americans. Detroit: Gale Research, 1995, pp. 64–65.

Terry, Wallace. "Success isn't what you have – It's what you've given away." *Parade Magazine,* June 2, 1996.

Viola, Herman J. *Ben Nighthorse Campbell, An American Warrior.* New York: Orion Books, 1993.

Wilma Mankiller: Chief of the Cherokee Nation

Ahearn, Lorraine. "Cherokee Leader Blazed A Hard Trail." *Greensboro News & Record,* March 3, 1995, page B1.

Chiu, Yvonne. "Former chief serves as a beacon of hope." *Dallas Morning News,* October 6, 1995, page 39A.

Glassman, Bruce. *Wilma Mankiller, Chief of the Cherokee Nation.* New York: The Rosen Publishing Group, 1992.

Mankiller, Wilma, and Michael Wallis. *Mankiller: A Chief and Her People.* New York: St. Martin's Press, 1993.

Notable Native Americans. Detroit: Gale Research, 1996, pp. 256–257.

Fred Begay: Navajo Nuclear Physicist

Easthouse, Keith. "The Long Walk of Fred Begay." *New Mexican,* May 9, 1993.

"The Long Walk of Fred Young." *Nova,* number 602, produced by BBC-TV, 1979.

McDowett, Bart. "New Mexico: Between Frontier and Future." *National Geographic,* November, 1987.

Notable Native Americans. Detroit: Gale Research, 1995, pp. 27–28.

Notable Twentieth-Century Scientists. Detroit: Gale Research, 1995, pp. 136–7.

St. John, Jetty. *Native American Scientists.* Mankato, MN: Capstone Press, 1996, pp. 22–27.

Stith, James H. *Physics Today:* vol. 49, Issue 7, July 1996, pp. 39–46.

ORLAND PARK PUBLIC LIBRARY